THE GABRIELINO

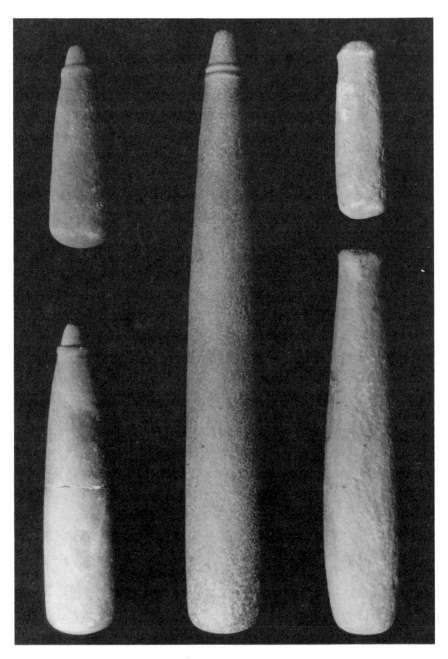

Pestles. Collection of Mr. Carl Hegner. San Nicolàs Island. Courtesy Southwest Museum.

THE GABRIELINO

WRITTEN AND ILLUSTRATED BY

BRUCE W. MILLER

1991
SAND RIVER PRESS
LOS OSOS, CALIFORNIA

BOOKS BY THE SAME AUTHOR

Chumash, A Picture of Their World.
The Caner's Handbook
Handmade Silkflowers

Copyright © Bruce W. Miller III

Published by SAND RIVER PRESS.
1319 14th street
Los Osos, CA., 93402

Copies of this book can be obtained by sending $7.95 + 1.50 postage and handling to: Sand River Press, 1319 14th street, Los Osos, CA., 93402.
CALIFORNIA RESIDENTS PLEASE ADD 7.25% SALES TAX.

FIRST PRINTING

10 9 8 7 6 5 4 3

Printed in the United States of America.

This book for Leslie Michele Simone, who saved my life.
Dance and be wonderful!

Love, half angel and half bird,
and all a wonder and a wild desire.

ROBERT BROWNING

ACKNOWLEDGEMENTS

I would like to thank Mike Cowdrey, Michele Simone, Mark Hall-Patton and Ken Kenyon for manuscript corrections and copy editing. I am grateful to Christopher Gibson for his publishable corrections and his unpublishable addition of the Tractatus to the manuscript. I am also indebted to the Southwest Museum, Bob Klyver: the Pacific Coast Archaeological Society and Jane Gothold; Antelope Valley Indian Museum and Edra Moore for access and photographic use of their Gabrielino collections, the Natural History Museum of Los Angeles County. I would like to thank the scholars and field archeologists whose fine and noteworthy research has made this book possible. John Peabody Harrington, H. E. Bolton, Fernando Librado, A.L. Kroeber, Thomas C. Blackburn, Travis Hudson, Bruce Bryan, Walter Ebeling, Bernice Eastman Johnston and many others.

TABLE OF CONTENTS

Ceremonial sandstone bowl and pestle from the cairns at Chatsworth. Courtesy Southwest Museum.

BEGINNINGS

THE GABRIELNO WERE NAMED by the Spanish for the Mission San Gabriel. It was an arbitrary naming, but one that stuck and it is servicable here. They are a magnificent people with a profound cultural heritage. They deserve our respect and attention. Here then is some of their story.

Solid dating for the Gabrielino area begins around 6000 B. C. with proven habitation for at least seven thousand years. Whether the most ancient of these people were direct forbears of the historical Gabrielino is uncertain. Most researchers believe that the Gabrielino, a branch of Shoshonean speaking people, drove a wedge through the Southern California desert to the sea, driving out and separating peoples of the Hokan family about two thousand years ago. The Gabrielino had come from the Great Basin, which makes up most of Southern Oregon and Nevada. This was probably not a mass migration but a series of small incursions over many years. This drive to the sea was stimulated by the relative fertility of the land into which they pushed, land that was a great deal more hospitable than the deserts of Nevada and the Eastern Sierra (Terrell 1979:146).

In any case, they adapted to their environment and had much in common with their Hokan speaking neighbors to the north, the Chumash. For the Gabrielino this was a time of great change. As the population shifted, ways changed. New types of food were brought into the diet. Acorns became more important, and those groups that made it to the coast harvested the sea. The Gabrielino learned to use the mortar and pestle from other coastal tribes.

We know that they liked to live on the high ground in the shelter of oak trees, on the open coastal plains, along the banks of coastal rivers, and at the seashore. They were predominantly a coastal people although many villages were scattered in the greater Los Angeles Basin, north to Topanga Canyon and south along the coast past Laguna Beach. Stand at the shoreline in Long Beach and the Gabrielino inhabited the land and sea for fifty miles in any direction. The territory circumscribed 4000 square miles, with the Los Angeles and Santa Ana Rivers running through its heart. The great transverse ranges, the San Gabriel Mountains and the San Bernardino Mountains, were marked barriers to their land.

Their villages were bunched along the shore near Long Beach and had exotic-sounding placenames: Tovemungna, Harasngna, Kingingna, Xujungna, Munikangna, and Suangna. Out to sea were the Channel Islands, named by the Spanish: Santa Catalina, San Clemente, San Nicolàs, and Santa Barbara. These too were Gabrielino territory. The four upper Channel Islands were held by the Chumash, their friendly neighbors.

The natural landscape of the Gabrielino was rich and varied from the mountain regions of the San Gabriels to the rolling plains of Los Angeles Basin. In their new territory, they earned a living by gathering roots and seeds, and fruit; fishing and harvesting shellfish; hunting mostly small animals, and occasionally the antelope and deer which roamed the wilderness. They built large village sites with thatched houses and plank canoes for fishing and for travel to the Channel Islands. By 500 A. D. the Gabrielino reached a high point in bone, shell and stone technology with advanced fishing and hunting abilities. They fashioned elegant bone whistles, incised pendants, and made sand and rock paintings. They used shell beads to decorate hairpins and made sophisticated shell jewelry, fishhooks and finely woven baskets.

Unlike their northern neighbors the Chumash, the Gabrielino practiced cremation form of burial, rather than inhumation. This, in part, accounts for the relative lack of archaeological evidence in the Gabrielino area. Like many of their Southern California neighbors, they practiced the Great Mourning Ceremony, based on the belief that there was an afterlife where much of what had been used in this life would be needed again. Weapons, clothing, and household implements were ritualistically *killed*, or broken so the spirit of the object could leave and join the dead person in the next world.

For a long time before the Gabrielino immigration the Channel Islands had been occupied and a full-time expansive maritime orientation was in swing. The Islands may have been occupied as far back as 10,000 years, though this may represent a food gathering presence and not a permanent occupation. Radiocarbon dates from San Nicolàs Island indicate that it was heavily populated between 2500 and 4000 years ago by a resourceful and imaginative people. Early adventurers describe the whole west end of San Nicolàs Island as being a vast kitchen midden ten feet high and more than a mile in length (Johnson:1962,107).

The Gabrielino probably learned to build plank canoes from the Chumash, but soon they became masters of the art of canoe building, and for good reason. They had at their disposal an almost inexhaustible supply of shark, sardines, yellow tail, bonito, and halibut. They also developed a trading economy among themselves and with their neighbors. Intratribal trade with the Island Gabrielino included seeds, deer hide, and rabbit skin for which the mainlanders received steatite either in raw chunks or fashioned into digging stick weights, ollas, pipes and effigies. Trade also flourished between nearby groups; the Chumash to the north, the Cahuilla and Mojave to the east and the Juaneño, and Luiseño to the south. This trade was frequently beneficial to all, so that a Southern California trading economy based on craft specialization developed, making the Gabrielino second in wealth only to the Chumash in all of California.

They were also culturally rich, with their own music, art and cosmology. They made beautiful sand paintings whose meaning is still a mystery. They developed a strong sense of community and self. They had a highly developed sense of ritual and spiritual power which manifested itself in their daily life. Above all, they had a vibrant and relatively peaceful existence.

Feather and bone hairpin.

HISTORY

EUROPEAN INTRUSION INTO THE LAND of the Gabri-
elino began in 1542, when the Cabrillo expedition *discovered* California. This first contact from the outside world signaled the end
of one era and the beginning of a new one. A new reality had come
to the Gabrielino. Though little changed by this first visit, the
Indians almost certainly took this event as significant, for the
Spanish explorers must have seemed truly powerful to them. Here
is the story of that first visit.

The purpose of Cabrillo's voyage, which started at Navidad, Mexico on the 27th of June, was to explore the coast of New
Spain and look for a new route to China. Three months into the
voyage he had sailed far enough north to discover Alta California
and a small land-locked port which he named San Miguel. Later
this port became known as San Diego.

Juan Rodriguez Cabrillo left San Diego Bay on October
3rd, and sailed north up the coast. Four days later he sighted San
Clemente and Santa Catalina Islands. These were named San Salvador and La Victoria after the expedition's small Spanish caravels. Dropping anchor at San Pedro Bay, a small sheltered cove at
Catalina, the explorers were met by numerous Indians who were

alarmed at first. Later, after signs of appeasement were made, the natives came off shore in a small plank canoe.

> *They [Cabrillo] gave them beads and other articles, with which they were pleased and then they returned. Afterwards the Spaniards went ashore, and they, the Indian women and all felt very secure. Here an old Indian made signs to them that men like the Spaniards, clothed and bearded, were going about on the mainland. They remained on the Island until midday (Bolton 1908: 24).*

Early the next day the two ships left the Islands and headed back toward the mainland.

Cabrillo stood on the deck of his flag ship *San Salvador* casting his eye to the continent ahead. There he spotted numerous fires from villages along the shoreline. He motioned his crew to change course and find anchor in the bay, probably present day San Monica. The consort ship *La Victoria* followed close behind. Because of the many campfires, Cabrillo named the bay, *La Bahia de los Fumos*, "The Bay of Smokes"

Cabrillo, an intrepid explorer in search of fame and fortune was sailing under the flag of Spain. His chief pilot, Bartolome Ferrelo, motioned to the crew of conscripts and Baja California Indian natives to drop anchor, and moments later it splashed into the water and sank to the sandy bottom. Now in the protected waters of the bay, they trimmed the sails and discussed whether to make landfall. The Southern California sun and fine Mediterranean weather reminded Cabrillo of his homeland. Above, the gold and crimson banner of Imperial Spain unfurled in the stiff coastal breeze. In the end they decided not to go ashore.

The next day, Cabrillo raised anchor and sailed north out of Gabrielino territory into the Santa Barbara Channel to be greeted by the Chumash. They passed the three largest of the Channel Islands, which Cabrillo mistook for one large Island. Cabrillo handed out presents to the Chumash and in return the Indians gave the Spanish *many fresh and very good sardines* (Bolton 1916).

Cabrillo continued up the Channel with good winds until he reached Cape Galera, (Point Concepcion). Here trouble started, when storms and rough weather buffeted the two ships compelling them to take refuge at wind-swept San Miguel Island for a week. Further tragedy struck when Cabrillo fell and broke his arm near the shoulder, an injury which later caused his death.

The storm let up slightly, but Cabrillo was in great pain and the crew were miserable from the rough weather. They were driven about off the mainland until finally making anchor at the *rancheria*, [village] *Las Sardinas* (Gaviota Pass) where food, water and wood were at hand, thanks to the friendly Chumash.

In spite of the pain of his broken bone, Cabrillo, and his intrepid crew set sail north. On the way they met another storm, and the two caravels separated. *San Salvador* and the *La Victoria* continued on separately and the *San Salvador* recorded its farthest point north as 39 degrees and 31 minutes (Fort Ross), on November 11. Four days later, heading south, they sighted the consort *La Victoria* and Cabrillo's crew rejoiced. On the southern leg of their journey they named the Sierra Nevadas, and *Bahia de los Piño*s (Drake's Bay).

Rounding Point Concepcion, they again harbored at San Miguel Island and there passed the winter. On January 3, 1543, Juan Rodriguez Cabrillo, explorer and captain of the flagship *San Salvador*, died from his injury.

Bartolome Ferrelo, a native of Levant and chief navigator, was designated as captain by the failing Cabrillo, who charged him not to leave off exploring. Ferrelo voyaged north but met with storms again, so he quickly returned, taking refuge in what is now Smugglers Cove at Santa Cruz Island. Ferrelo commented:

The Indians of these islands are very poor. They are fishermen and eat nothing except fish. They live in houses that can hold fifty people and go about naked (Englehardt 1923:11).

Meanwhile, the bad weather separated the caravels again and the *La Victoria* struck some shoals on San Miguel Island. The crew, thinking they were lost, stripped most of their clothes off and promised the Blessed Virgin that if saved they would make a pilgrimage to the nearest church. The *San Salvador* sailed south to *Las Canoas*, a Chumash village, and waited. Later, it sailed south to Gabrielino territory and on to San Diego. When finally the *La Victoria* appeared, there was much celebrating and the two Spanish caravels set sail, arriving at their starting point, La Navidad, on Saturday, April 14th, 1543, where the sailors of the *La Victoria* made good their vow.

The next significant visitor to the area was Sebastian Vizcáino, who sixty years later on May 5th, 1602, set sail from Acapulco with three ships, *San Diego*, *Santo Tomás*, a Peruvian galleon and *Tres Reyes*, locally built. His mission was to survey and explore the California coast and to make maps of possible ports. Theirs was a journey of great hardship, in small, badly-fitted ships easily buffeted by any passing storm. The crew often had little to eat and scurvy was prevalent (Johnson:1962,98).

On November 20th, *Tres Reyes* raised anchor at San Diego and sailed north, ahead of the other two ships. *San Diego* and *Santo Tomás*, both larger vessels followed at a more leisurely pace surveying and mapmaking. They soon passed San Clemente Island and then dropped anchor at Santa Catalina. There they were met by many Indians paddling plank canoes.

With Vizcáino were three Carmelite Fathers, Fr. Andres de la Asumpcion, Fr. Antonio de la Ascencion, and Fr. Tomás de Aquino. Father Ascencion's commission on the voyage was that of second chaplain and as an assistant to cosmographer, Geronimo Martin Palacios. Ascencion's primary mission, a task he set for himself, was the evangelization and pacification of all the natives of California (Aschman 176). In his journal of the voyage Father Ascencion wrote:

After we left San Diego we discovered many islands in a line, one after another. Most of them are inhabited by many friendly Indians who have trade with those of the mainland. From the mainland a petty chief came with his son and eight oarsman to visit us, saying that he would entertain us and provide us with anything we needed and he possessed. The petty chief seeing that there were no women on board then offered by signs to give everyone ten women apiece if they would all go to his land, which shows you how thickly populated it is (Bolton: 1925,118).

Father Ascencion and three other men went ashore at Santa Catalina to visit a nearby *rancheria* at the behest of the native chief. There the explorers saw an enclosure of a sort of *temple* surrounded with bird feathers. On opposite sides of this area were paintings of the sun and the moon (Johnson:1962,99).

On the 27th of the month they dropped anchor in a very good cove where a multitude of Indians came out in canoes of cedar and pine, made of planks very well joined and caulked, each one with eight oars and with fourteen or fifteen Indians, who looked like galley slaves. They came alongside without the slightest fear and came on board our ships, mooring their own. They showed great pleasure at seeing us, telling us by signs that we must land, and guiding us like pilots to the anchorage. The General received them kindly and gave them some presents, especially to the boys. We anchored, and the admiral, Ensign Alarcon, Father Fray Antonio, and Captain Peguero, and some soldiers, went ashore. Many Indians were on the beach, and the women treated us to roasted sardines and small fruit like sweet potatoes.

The next day the General and the Father Commissary went ashore, a hut was built, and mass was said. More than one hundred and fifty Indian men and women were present, and they marvelled not a little at seeing the altar and the image of our Lord Jesus crucified, and listened attentively to the saying of mass, asking by signs what it was all about. When the divine service was ended the General went to their houses, where the women took him by the hand and led him inside, giving him some food which they had given before. He brought to the ship six Indian girls from eight to ten years old, whom their mothers willingly gave him, and he clothed them with chemises, petticoats and necklaces and sent them ashore. The rest of the women, seeing this, came with their daughters in canoes, asking for gifts. The result was that no one returned empty-handed. The people go dressed in seal skins, the women especially covering their loins, and their faces show them to be modest; but the men are thieves, for anything they saw unguarded they took. They are a people given to trade and traffic and are fond of barter, for in return for old clothes they would give the soldiers, skins, shells, nets, thread, and very well twisted ropes, these in great quantity and resembling linen (Bolton: 1908,84).

Santa Catalina Island. Cartography by Enrico Martinez, 1603.

Several days later Vizcáino raised anchor, crossing over to the mainland where he went ashore at San Pedro Bay. There he instructed the Gabrielino Indians in Christian dogma and placed a cross on a native idol which...*resembled a demon, having two horns, no head, a dog at its feet and many children painted all around it. The Indians told the General not to go near it, but he approached it and saw the whole thing, and made a cross and placed the name of Jesus on the head of the demon (Bolton 1908:85).*

[Nearly all of the Spanish explorers were blind to the richness of American Indian religious traditions. Here was a clear case of Vizcáino desecrating a Gabrielino shrine. This stands in stark contrast to the respect, and courtesy which the Gabrielino had shown toward Spanish religious customs.]

On the first day of December, Vizcáino's small fleet left San Pedro Bay and sailed north in heavy fog. When the fog lifted, they sighted two islands which they named San Nicolàs and Santa Barbara. From here, they sailed on into Chumash territory and then even further north, finally reaching Mendocino. There, in heavy weather, on January 17, Vizcáino was injured when a crate of provisions broke loose from its berth fracturing several of his ribs. Three days later they turned south and by January 25 were again at Monterey Bay. Heading south they again passed Santa Catalina. Since they were very short of water and supplies, it was decided that they would not anchor but go on in search of provisions, and so passed out of Gabrielino territory for the second and last time. The expedition reached Acapulco on March 22, 1603.

It is surprising that for the next 166 years that the Gabrielino were left in peace for no other outside visitor touched their shores. Other navigators may have visited the Channel Islands, or the mainland but there is no record of them doing so.

On July 14, 1769, Don Gaspar de Portolá, heading a party of sixty-four men on the first land expedition to New California, left San Diego. Portolá was a bachelor at midlife and in his prime. A career officer in the army, he had once fought in Italy and

Portugal before finding service in New Spain. Now, he was the man who was given the task of establishing Spain's claim on the territory of *Neuva California*. This was to be done, first, by exploring and secondly, by establishing permanent settlements much in the fashion that had been used in Mexico over the previous two hundred years.

Portolá went first by horseback to San Diego. From there, he travelled northward with a pack train of one hundred and eighty animals and sixty-four men, a column that stretched out for a full kilometer behind him. Scouts were in front, then Commander Portolá, followed by Ensign Miguel Costansó and in turn Lieutenant Pedro Fages, and a half-dozen soldiers dressed in six-ply, deerskin vests, each carrying a sword, a musket and a lance. Then, perhaps, came two Franciscan friars on mules, Juan Crespí and Francisco Gomez. Behind them was a hundred-animal pack train with a dozen mounted drivers alongside and bringing up the rear were the rest of the animals and a company of soldiers (Squibb 1984).

Crespí, Fages, and Costansó all kept journals and it is from those records that we get a glimpse of the Gabrielino before the Spanish began to alter their world (Grant 1965).

Four days after setting out from San Diego, the explorers reached a pleasant valley, where Mission San Luis Rey would later be built. Progress was slow because of the task of erecting and breaking camp each day. Water had to be located and meals prepared. On a normal day they made three or four leagues, (9-12 miles).

As they entered Gabrielino territory they were welcomed by friendly Indians. On the 22nd of July they were permitted to baptize two dying children, who were named by the priests Maria and Margarita. They noticed that Indians had burned many grassy areas to facilitate the capture of rabbits and the growth of chia sage.

Portolá's expedition carried with them a good supply of trade beads and ribbons, which they exchanged for baskets, feather work and animal skins. To eat, they were given dried fish, acorns, pinole, chia (sage seeds), and other cooked foods.

On the 24th, San Clemente and Santa Catalina islands were sighted. Several days later on the 28th, four violent earthquakes hit the area and frightened the Indians. Portolá and his party were crossing the Santa Ana River and so named the stream *Jesus de los Tremblores*. Costansó speaks of the Indian village nearby.

We pitched our camp on the left bank of the river. To the right there is a populous Indian village; the inhabitants received us with great kindness. Fifty-two of them came to our quarters and their captain asked us by signs which we understood easily, to remain there and live with them. [He said] that they would provide antelopes, hares, or seeds for our subsistence, that the lands which we saw were theirs, and they would share them with us (Teggart 1911:177).

Father Juan Crespí relates a similar story of this Indian chief who lived near present day Anaheim.

We told him that we would return and would gladly remain to live with them, and when the chief understood it he was so affected that he broke into tears. The governor made them a present of some beads and a small silk handkerchief, and in gratitude the chief gave us two baskets of seeds already made into pinole, together with a string of beads made of shells such as they wear (Bolton 1927:142).

The expedition continued west through mountains and canyons and along the desert watercourses. Costansó relates the events of those days:

We halted at this place which was called La Porciuncula. Here we felt three successive earthquakes during the afternoon and night.

We forded the Rio de la Porciuncula [Los Angeles River] which descends with great rapidity from the canyon through which it leaves the mountains and enters the plains. All the country that we saw on this days march appeared to us most suitable for the production of all kinds of grain and fruit. On our way we met the entire population of an Indian village engaged in harvesting seeds on the plain (Teggart 1911:181).

Crespí adds:

Some of the old men were smoking pipes well made of baked clay and they puffed at us three mouthfuls of smoke. We gave them a little tobacco and glass beads, and they went away well pleased...After crossing the river we entered a large vineyard of wild grapes and an infinity of rosebushes in full bloom...After traveling about half a league we came to the village of this region, the people of which on seeing us, came out into the road. As they drew near they began to howl like wolves; they greeted us and wished to give us seeds, but we did not accept them. Seeing this, they threw some handfuls of them on the ground and the rest in the air (Bolton 1927:147).

The next day, August 4, Costansó states that they *found an Indian village and the inhabitants were very good natured. They came at once to our quarters with trays of seeds, nuts, and acorns; to these presents we responded with strings of glass beads, which they hold in high esteem* (Teggart 1911: 183).

Heading north and west, the expedition found abundant game and shot some antelope for fresh meat. They were now nearing the northern edge of Gabrielino territory. Ahead of them was the calm expanse of the Santa Barbara Channel and the territory of the Chumash Indians.

On the 8th and 9th of August they traveled steadily west and northwest, making their way through the canyons towards the sea. Costansó tells of their adventures:

In the afternoon, seven chiefs or caciques came with a large following of Indians armed with bows and arrows, but with the bow-strings loosened in sign of peace. They brought generous presents of seeds, acorns, nuts and pine-nuts, which they spread out before us, The chiefs inquired who was in command of us, and offered to the commander and his officers, as a mark of distinction, various necklaces of little black and white stones; in hardness and substance greatly resemble coral only differ from it in color. Today we have probably seen five hundred Indians (Teggart 1911:191).

For the rest of the week, they traveled northwest up and down the hills and gullies and across the plains of the mainland coast. They soon passed over the San Gabriel foothills into the San Fernando Valley and then headed north out of Gabrielino territory (Bancroft 1884:45).

To the north, Portolá was unable to recognize Monterey Bay, from Vizcáino's brief description, but he traveled far enough to discover San Francisco Bay. Portolá returned along the same route in the winter of 1770 somewhat dispirited after missing his supply ship at Monterey, and on January 24th, they arrived back at the little outpost of San Diego. All in all it was a relatively trouble-free trek of some twelve hundred miles.

This historic journey marked the beginning of the end for the Gabrielino Indians. And the man who was to change their lives more than anyone before or since this time was waiting at San Diego. His name was Father Junipero Serra. In the spring of 1770, Portolá set out from San Diego on another trek north through Gabrielino territory, again looking for Monterey bay. He found it in May of that year. A month later, Father Serra sailed north to Monterey to establish the second mission in *Alta California—San Carlos de Monterey*. It was then, that he would start mapping out the fate of the Gabrielino.

Steatite seal effigy (above) Dog effigy (below) found on San Nicolàs Island. Note the shell bead inlay eyes. Courtesy Catalina Island Museum.

THE MISSION ERA

SAN GABRIEL WAS THE NORTHERN most of four missions established under the jurisdiction of the presidio at San Diego. In 1770, Junipero Serra was commissioned to establish a chain of missions from San Diego to San Francisco Bay. Father Serra and Captain Pedro Fages, one of the military commanders along on the Portolá Expedition agreed that a mission should be established at the site of *Jesus de los Temblores*, where the expedition had experienced a sudden and heavy quake and numerous smaller aftershocks in 1769.

It fell to Fathers Somera and Cambón, who had come to San Diego by way of Monterey to establish Mission San Gabriel. They set out northward and traveled forty leagues in the company of ten soldiers and a number of packmules. Arriving at the *Rio de los Temblores* (San Gabriel River) they found a thicket of sycamore, ash, and willow and it was decided that the mission would be built on that spot (Dakin:1978, 263).

Hugo Reid, a Scotchman, well-known for his interest in Indian affairs, particularly Indians of the Los Angeles Basin described the area of the mission as a "complete forest of oaks..." with a thicket of "wild rose and wild grapevines" underneath.

A great number of Gabrielino and several tribal elders gathered as the founding party approached the area. Zephyrin Englehardt, a church historian describes the scene:

Fearing that a battle might ensue and that some might be killed, one of the fathers produced a canvas picture of Our Lady of Sorrows and put it in view of the savages. No sooner had he done this than all, overcome by the sight of the beautiful image, threw down their bows and arrows. The two Chiefs quickly ran up to lay at the feet of the Sovereign Queen as tokens of their greatest esteem the beads they wore on the neck. By the same action they manifested their desire to be at peace with us (Engelhardt 1927:4).

Thus, the mission was founded on good terms. All together, the Franciscan fathers founded twenty-one missions with two falling in the Gabrielino territory, Mission San Fernando and Mission San Gabriel.

The Franciscan priests, of course, thought they had the Indian's interest at heart; theirs was a utopian vision. It was their intention that the Indians would be drawn into the mission system, baptized, taught trades, and then released to be productive citizens. It was thought that this would take approximately a decade, after which the Indians would be given farmland and lead the lives of good Christians. Good intentions, however, are not always manifested in history.

Travel through Gabrielino territory was still infrequent, but around this time in 1774, Captain Juan Bautista de Anza set out on the first of two overland expeditions to upper California. The purpose of the first expedition was to find a good land route from Sonora to Monterey, which he did, and to bring with him settlers, sheep and cattle in support of the Mission system.

The first Anza expedition left Tubac, a presidio south of present-day Tucson, Arizona, in January 1774, with thirty-four men. They moved north and crossed the Colorado River with the aid of the Yuma Indians. Heading immediately in to the harsh southern desert they became mired and lost for six days in large sand dunes. Struggling back to the Colorado River, their animals dying at a rapid rate, the expedition recuperated while the animals were set to pasture. Setting out once again, they headed west along what is now the Mexican border, passing through the Anza Desert and Borrego Valley and over the mountains through Royal Pass. By March 22, they had reached Mission San Gabriel, which had been founded a scant three years earlier and which now provided safe refuge, although little food as the mission was in the midst of its own famine.

The Anza expedition continued north along the coast stopping at the new Mission San Luis Obispo de Tolosa and then went on to Monterey. Along the way, Anza was generous with trade beads and smoking tobacco, spreading them liberally among the Indians. He also made careful maps, noting the fertility of the soil and availability of fresh water (Grant 1965), (Bolton 1930).

The second Anza expedition began in 1775 and is primarily important for its founding of the mission at San Francisco. The settlement of San Francisco was an attempt by the Spanish to stop the Southerly advance of the Russians.

This second expedition consisted of a small group of soldiers attached to Anza and another thirty soldiers with wives and children who intended to remain in California as *pobladores*, or settlers. Altogether with Fathers Font, Garces, Eixarch, servants, muleteers, cattle drivers, families, and soldiers, the expedition numbered some two hundred and forty people. Over one thousand domestic animals were taken including nearly seven hundred horses and mules and three hundred and fifty beef cattle. The cattle were used for subsistence enroute and for breeding stock at the new settlements, particularly San Francisco. The Anza expedition nearly doubled the domestic animal population in Alta California (Bean 1973).

Father Pedro Font, acting in the capacity of chaplain and

chronicler of the expedition, left a journal which is informative. In it he provides information about the landscape and the native Americans whom he encountered. He was not afraid to speak his mind and was a fearless observer, much more so than his contemporary Fr. Juan Crespí.

On January 1, 1776, the Anza Expedition forded *Río de Santa Ana* (Santa Ana River) and camped for the night. They reached Mission San Gabriel on the 4th where Font entered this passage in his diary.

The mission of San Gabriel is situated about eight leagues from the sea, in a most beautiful and ample place with plenty of water and very good soil. The site is level and open and about two leagues from the Sierra Nevada, which lies to the north—we had this range on our right since leaving Puerto de San Carlos. At the mission we found Captain Fernando de Rivera y Moncada, who had come here on his way to the presidio of San Diego on account of the rising of the San Diego Mission Indians, who destroyed it, and killed its minister, Father Jaume (Font 1913:43).

The next night Font went to observe the Mission San Gabriel aqueduct. He remarked: *I went with Fr. Sanchez to see the spring of water from which they run the aqueduct to this Mission of San Gabriel, by means of which it is provided with the best conveniences for besides being an ample water course, it passes in front of the dwelling of the fathers and the little huts of the Christian Indians who compose the new Mission. Of these there may be, big and little, five hundred souls of recent converts (Englehardt 1927:30).*

On that same day, January 5, Font also wrote of what he observed of the Native Americans living near the mission boundary: *The Indian converts of this mission, who are of the Beñeme nation and also of the Jeniguechi [Gabrielino] tribe, appear to be peaceful and of somewhat good heart. They are of medium stature, but the women are somewhat smaller, round faced, flat nosed and somewhat ugly. The men in their pagan state are accustomed to go entirely naked, but the women wear some sort of deer skin with which they cover themselves and also a kind of small cloak of otter or rabbit skins (Engelhardt 1927:34).*

Hearing of the revolt at San Diego, Anza split his expedition, leaving the civilians at San Gabriel and took some of his soldiers and Font to San Diego with Commander Rivera (Bancroft 1884:265). They moved fast and arrived at San Diego on the January Eleventh. There they set about trying to find the natives responsible for the uprising. Many had fled to the mountains but some were captured and punished. There were investigations and it wasn't until Feb. 11th that Anza, his soldiers and Fr. Pedro Font arrived back at San Gabriel to continue their journey north.

In general, the Gabrielino Indians were peaceful but Fr. Font did make the observation that the women of the villages ran and hid when the Spanish approached. He laid this to the abuse that they had suffered from the soldiers in the past.

The expedition ended on March 29, 1776, with the founding of the Mission San Francisco de Asis by the side of a creek which Anza named *Laguna de Nuestra Senora de los Dolores* from which the popular name Mission Dolores arose. This was the sixth in the chain of California missions that was slowly being forged by the Spanish like shackles, to bind the California Indian population.

Life in the missions was a vast change for the Gabrielino. For the most part, the new converts—neophytes as they were called, were camped around the missions, away from their traditional village sites. They were taught by the priests to abandon their native ways, and were instead forced to learn the basic trades to establish the mission economy. The Indians were taught tile-making, woodworking, agriculture, weaving, animal husbandry, metal forging, and leather crafts. The women worked in the shops, spinning, weaving and sewing everything from shirts to pantaloons. Moccasins and jackets were made of leather and blankets were woven of wool. The men dug the irrigation ditches, tended the crops, plowed the fields and constructed the buildings. Both sexes harvested the crops. However, with few exceptions, they were not taught to read, beyond a few musical notes for fear the education would promote dissention and strife among them.

The daily routine was prescribed in detailed, written regulations which the Indians were made to follow unwaveringly. If they did not, food was withheld, or the lash applied. When girls reached the age of eleven they were kept with the other single women and those whose husbands had fled, in the *monjerio*, or nunnery.

The day began at first light. A bell was tolled and all the Indians over the age of ten were to appear at Mass. After services, the Indians were instructed in the Spanish language then released for breakfast. Unattached men and women were not allowed to eat together but had to go to their respective quarters (Terrell 1976).

The mission economy was maintained by native labor. With the profits from selling products to the presidios, settlers, and Yankee traders, the priests bought metals—primarily iron—as well as cloth, and tools. Some profits went to embellishments for the mission chapels—statues, religious goods, crucifixes and occasionally trinkets for the Indians.

Each year the mission fathers appointed an Indian *alcaldes*. These *alcaldes* were not necessarily chosen from the Gabrielino elite and hence owed their new-found power to the mission priests rather than the traditional Gabrielino elders. Thus, one more way was found to enhance the mission system: alter the power base, and a new group benefits, while the old erodes.

The missions were meant to be self-sustaining, and to provide a completely new life for the neophytes. The men were given a pair of breeches and a shirt; the women a skirt. In return, the Indians were made to build the presidios and missions, including the high walls that surrounded them at night.

As time progressed and Mission San Gabriel flowered, more settlers crowded into the Los Angeles Basin. A settlement was called for and so on September 4, 1781, an expedition set out from San Gabriel Mission to found the City of Los Angeles, called *El*

Pueblo de la Reina de Los Angeles. There was a detachment of soldiers and forty-four settlers, including twenty-two children. Englehardt states that:

> The plaza had already been laid out, and the boundaries fixed for the building lots that faced it. As they neared the selected spot, a procession was formed made up of the soldiers, with the governor (Felipe de Neve) at their head, the priests from San Gabriel, accompanied by their Indian acolytes, then the male settlers, and lastly, women and the children, the former bearing a large banner of the Virgin Mary painted upon it. The procession marched slowly and impressively around the plaza, followed, no doubt, by the wondering gaze of the Indians of Yang-na, who had assembled for the event. (Yang-na was the name that the Indians in that area of a Los Angeles Basin called themselves.)

The colony thrived, although with some disorder, and by 1790, the pueblo produced more grain than any mission in California except its neighbor Mission San Gabriel. Los Angeles then had twenty nine building, including a public town hall, guardhouse, and granaries.

The early years of Mission San Gabriel were a time of enormous change for the Gabrielino. Within thirteen years of the mission's founding, over a thousand Indians had been baptised. But the natives suffered terribly under the Spanish, particularly from the soldiers, who used the Gabrielino women badly, much to the disgust of the mission fathers. The Indian men were forced to labor, constructing the adobe mission, and the surrounding settlements; and both sexes were forced to work the fields, raising what the Spanish considered proper foods. This new diet of strachy grain, and occasionally beef, wreaked havoc with the health of the Gabrielino. Combined with the lack of sanitation caused by restricted living conditions forced upon them by the Spanish, their unhealthy diet led to many deaths. Lacking any immunity to European diseases, such as tuberculosis, pneumonia, chicken pox, measles, smallpox, and syphilis, the Gabrielino were defenseless. Their numbers dwindled, the average life span dropped precipitously, to six or seven years. Misery encompassed them all, men, women, and children. They died of European enlightenment— hard work, diseases, and an unaccustomed diet.

So it isn't surprising that in October of 1785, soldiers at the San Gabriel Mission narrowly avoided open bloodshed when a number of the Gabrielino rose up in revolt. Englehardt gives this account of the abortive resurrection.

In October 1785, the neophytes and gentiles were tempted by a woman, so at least the men said, into a plan to attack the Mission and kill the friars. The corporal in command prevented the success of the scheme without bloodshed, and captured some twenty conspirators. Fages hurried south from the capitol, put the four ringleaders in prison to await the decision of the commandant-general, and released the rest with fifteen or twenty lashes each. Two years later came General Ugarte's orders condemning one native, Nicolas, to six years work at the presidio followed by exile to a distant Mission. The woman was sent into perpetual exile, and the other two were dismissed with the two years' imprisonment already suffered (Englehardt 1927:61), (Bancroft 1884:459,460).

Again, in 1810, some three dozen Gabrielino were remanded for plotting a revolt. Twenty-one neophytes, and a dozen free Indians were sent to Santa Barbara to receive the lash for nine days straight. They were then made to do hard punishment.

A system of peonage was established at the missions. Indians were farmed out to the soldiers, or settlers to do whatever was needed, and in return, the mission was paid. This newly-trained work force was extremely valuable to the mission fathers, and they would not have been able to succeed had the Indians resisted.

Father Ramon Oblés, in answering one of the questionnaires (*Interrogatorios*) sent to the missions by the Spanish authorities in Mexico observed:

The people of this province, known as the gente de razon, (people of reason—whites), are so lazy and indolent that they know nothing more than how to ride horseback. Labor of any kind they regard as dishonorable. They are of the opinion that only the Indians ought to work; wherefore they solicit the service of the Indians for even the most necessary things for their maintenance such as cooking, washing, doing garden work, taking care of babies, etc. Generally the missionary Fathers let them have the Indians for work (Englehardt 1923:98).

Engelhardt believed that San Gabriel Mission was singularly unfortunate in having to contend from the first, with many degenerate soldiers, and outcasts from Mexico.

The responses (*respuestas*) which the Fathers made to the thirty-six questions put to them by the Spanish Government are illuminating in some respects and contain interesting information about the Gabrielino. The mission fathers themselves, although no doubt good observers of human nature, had little interest in any ethnographic reporting. Hence, much of what could have been observed and recorded has been lost forever. The one great exception in the case of the Gabrielino is Boscana whose extraordinary essay, Chinigchinich, has given us much useful information. One should, of course, remember that anthropology didn't become a bonafide science until the 1870's so Boscana was clearly ahead of his time. Still, there are a good many diaries, journals, letters and *interrogatorios* of various sorts, made by the priests, settlers, Yankee traders, and civil and military authorities. These provide a window by which one gets an imperfect view of the Gabrielino: a sort of historical glimpse full of natural bias but nonetheless an honest account from the diarist's perspective. In the absence of better sources these must do.

Hugo Reid, a chronicler of Gabrielino history, had much to say on these early meetings between the Spanish colonizers and the natives of the Los Angeles Basin. In 1852, towards the end of his life he wrote a number of letters (really sketches) for a newspaper called the *Los Angeles Star*. These letters made a significant impact and were read with great interest in Southern California and elsewhere. In all twenty-two letters were published and they are a fine source of information on the Gabrielino Indians. They are most commonly available as an appendix to Susanna Bryant Dakin's *A Scotch Paisano in Old Los Angeles* (University of California 1939, 1978). Reid was married to native American (Doña Victoria)

He had much to say about the Gabrielinos' treatment at the hands of the Spanish colonist and the mission fathers. Reid provides us with a good antidote to Zephyrin Englehardt's pious views. Englehardt, the official Church biographer, of course, had his own ideas as to the treatment of the Indians and goes so far as to call Reid that "soured Scotchman" (Englehardt 1927:354).

Also in 1824, Mexico declared itself free of Spain and the liberal-minded new government framed the Federal Constitution of the United Mexican States, modelling their document after the Constitution of the United States.

This same year the Chumash, the northern neighbors who in general suffered the same fate as the Gabrielino with respect to the Spanish, revolted. This revolt was vastly more successful than the Gabrielino revolt of 1785 and involved three missions (Santa Barbara, La Purísima Concepción, and Santa Ynez) and as many as a thousand Chumash, many of whom fled to the central valley of California.

One of the first notions the new government put into practice was the secularization of the missions. In 1827, the Indians were declared free, and able to move at will. Having been taught domestic skills by the mission fathers, they were to go out and put these skills into practice and become useful citizens of the new republic. The mission fathers argued against secularization, because it would bring the vast mission lands under control of the government. It was also argued that the Indians were not ready for secularization. Some countered that after fifty years under the mission system they would never be ready. The two missions in Gabrielino territory controlled vast lands, vineyards, orchards, and many thousands of head of cattle, sheep and horses.

Full secularization of the missions, which began in 1833, meant another dramatic change for the California Indians. Private citizens were now given land grants over the territory previously owned by the Church (Grant 1965).

Governor Jose Figuroa's Provisional Regulations for the Emancipation of the Mission Indians, issued July 15, 1833, provided that half the land and property of the missions was to go to the Indians and half to the administrators. Many of these administrators were unscrupulous and failed to hold the property in trust for the Indians. The law forbade the Indians from disposing of their land, so many tried farming small plots for a few years but they quickly failed and gave up the effort. Some were dispossessed by trick, or by debt, and the mission lands fell into the hands of those holding the land grants or were subdivided into ranchos (Bean 1973).

Secularization didn't change the demands put upon the Gabrielino. They were still expected to work for little or no money (room and board) and they were hopelessly poor, with no education, or even allowed the chance of obtaining one. Thus, the space of a single lifetime, the Gabrielino nation, whose territory once stretched over a vast portion of the Los Angeles Basin and whose people numbered in the thousands were reduced to near extinction. Culturally and spiritually, they had very nearly ceased to exist (Grant 1965).

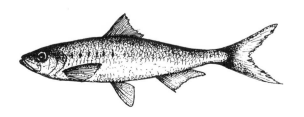

Three bone gorges and stone sinker strung on vegetal fiber string. Photograph Bruce W. Miller. Courtesy Antelope Valley Indian Museum.

AFTERMATH

THE CALIFORNIA MISSIONS, once great and powerful, fell into ruin. The lifelong dream of Father Serra came unraveled as the missions, one by one, were stripped of their land. As the missions died the Gabrielino scattered to the wind. Dispossessed of their traditional hunting lands and old village sites along the coast, the Gabrielino huddled around the remnants of the missions, or went to work on the vast ranchos as stock men and domestic servants. They also became urban dwellers, and moved into the poorest sections of a rapidly-growing Los Angeles barrio. Here, they came under the influence of liquor and vice. A few drifted away to join the interior tribes. In most cases, however, their old life was finished; the missions had changed that indelibly and forever. Stripped of their heritage and having abandoned their traditional beliefs they were culturally overwhelmed. And so the old ways of hunting and gathering were lost, many of the village elders were dead, or virtually underground, and fearful of public scrutiny. Their Shoshonean language skills had slipped into obsolescence. The special rituals and ceremonies of power had faded from importance in their lives. Things Gabrielino—actions, sand paintings, words, mythology, symbology were eclipsed or adulterated with Spanish and American ways. Families were separated, tribal life was discouraged, and Indians who sought the old ways were intimidated by constant harassment. Some social structure had existed under the missions. But now, the cultural fabric came unstitched as the Gabrielino tribe was further divided and absorbed by the Spanish settlements.

In the absence of their own culture, the Indians adopted the life of the rancho, but the Gabrielino fared no better in their freedom than they had under the bondage of the mission system. They merely changed masters from religious to secular, from mission to rancho. The ranchos provided some refuge, if hard work. In return for their labor, they received food and shelter but little else. A once proud, rich, and peaceful Indian nation, culturally and linguistically diverse, had been reduced by civilization to a dispirited and lost group of illiterate Christian laborers, no longer in control of their destiny (Margolin 1978).

California was rapidly changing and the ranchos were a sign of that change. This was the flowering of Mexican influence in California and for the land-grant Mexicans, the *Haciendadoes*, life was bountiful and easy, on their vast acreage. Time was spent herding cattle and sheep, and marketing hides and tallow from their livestock. Barbeques, fiestas, the vicious sport of bull and bear baiting, horsemanship, cockfighting and landed politics were the activities of the rancheros. The ranchos, however much like feudal kingdoms, were far from self-sufficient. In fact, much of what had been accomplished under the strict regime of the missions, in terms of agriculture and domestic arts, was lost during secularization. Some of this loss was due to deliberate destruction by the priests, who did not want to see their hard work fall into the hands of others, and some by neglect and laziness of the rancheros. Formerly, the missions had made coarse woolen blankets, shoes, saddles, soap, candles, and other basic supplies. Now much of this was made in New England, or in the Spanish settlements of Chile and Peru (Dana 1937), (Grant 1965).

The mission economy had produced a variety of agricultural products by the use of irrigation—wheat, barley, numerous fruits, and fresh vegetables, pumpkins, olive, muskmelons and grapes. On the ranchos, diet was beef—fresh, barbecued and jerked. Fresh milk, wheat flour, sugar, and molasses were used infrequently and considered luxuries. However, not withstanding the relative laziness and lack of industry on these sprawling ranchos, the owners and overlords did quite well (Bean 1973).

Though greatly romanticized, these halcyon days of the dons were just another trial to the Gabrielino. The Indians worked, and survived, and adapted as best they could under harsh circumstances. Living in extreme poverty, they were still abused and despised, especially by the whites, the American settlers—gringos, who were slowly infiltrating Mexican California.

Intermarriage between Mexicans and Indians became more common; while the pure-blooded natives slowly dwindled, due to old age, abuse, and disease. The mixed blood population increased. They learned to speak Spanish and later forgot the Shoshonean dialects they had spoken for millenia.

During the mission days, the Gabrielino had been allowed to leave the missions for brief durations to continue foraging for food, to hunt, and to visit their *rancherias*. This no doubt contributed to the continuation of their culture, in the short term. Increasingly, however, these villages ceased to exist, and the native population was culturally bereft. Gone were their lodges, their games, their beliefs, and their prosperous way of life (McCall & Perry, 1982). As the new generation grew up, they did with Mexican values, and Catholic religion.

The Island Gabrielino had long since disappeared, most having been rounded up by the Padres during the Mission Period.

This was also the era of the mountain men whose explorations into California from the East were pushing the western boundaries of the new nation. In 1833, the Joseph Reddeford Walker expedition came through the Sierras on their way to Monterey.

With him were a number of intrepid men including Zenas Leonard, Bill Williams and George Nidever. Nidever and Williams would later would later play an interesting part in Gabrielino history concerning the Lone Woman of San Nicolàs Island, some years later.

This group of mountain men was probably among the first outsiders to see the magnificent grandeur of the Yosemite Valley. Coming down the great Central Valley of California, they found a mixed group of mission Indians, mostly Chumash, who spoke Spanish, and farmed the land. These were probably neophytes who had fled the missions during the uprising in 1824. They had been joined by other fugitives, and prospered with their own cultural mixture of Spanish and traditional ways (Grant1965).

The Gabrielino too were becoming mixed with other tribes in the area. Indians from as far away as Mexico intermixed under the mission system, further destroying the unique tribal ways of the local culture. Still, some of the old ways managed to survive. Clamshell bead money was still being used, and baskets and steatite artifacts were still prized, and used on a daily basis.

Some Gabrielino were scattered throughout the mission system, as far north as the Monterey Peninsula and down into San Diego. Others went to live with the interior tribes, less under the control of the Spanish whose authority stopped within a twenty-five mile radius of Los Angeles.

The Gold Rush was an event which changed everything and sounded an ominous final toll for the Gabrielino and all California Indians for that matter. The Gold Rush, pushed by hundreds of thousands of fortune hunting Americans, changed California forever. It is estimated that more than fifty thousand Native Americans were slaughtered in just two short years. Between 1848 and 1850 the California Indians saw their number reduced by half. They were shot at, burned out, starved, harassed, jailed and murdered; or simply robbed and left to the neglect of the state. The mission Indians were seen by whites as a dispirited and impoverished lot, and were called diggers. The Americans, having stolen their land and erased their culture, largely ignored them, or placed them on reservations (Heizer 1974).

The Gabrielino, formerly one of the most-powerful and populous of the California tribes barely survived into the Twentieth Century.

CAPTURED HERITAGE

IN THE SECOND HALF of the Nineteenth Century, a new curiosity developed about Native American culture. This interest was not directed at the living Gabrielino, the few who were left, but towards the material relics of their decimated culture. This interest was not exclusively focused on the Gabrielino tribe, but was running rampant across most of the Western United States. Everywhere along the coast of North America, Indian artifacts were being crated up, and shipped out to museums at the four corners of the world. This was the beginning of the science of anthropology and the early days of field archaeology. In part, this acquisitive mania was a sign of the times. The Victorians were great collectors of every type of object, from Polynesian masks to Gabrielino effigies. Here was the apotheosis of Darwinian culture. Humanity defining itself thru its past—a noble and at times, tragic process.

The coast of California was no exception and as early as 1870, the shovels and dirt started to fly. In 1873, there were no less than three expeditions working along the Southern California coast. They mostly worked in Chumash territory to the north of the Los Angeles and on the Channel Islands, though San Nicolàs Island, a major Gabrielino site was excavated by several groups.

First to arrive was an expedition headed by Paul Schumacher, under the greater auspices of the Smithsonian Institution and the Peabody Museum. Shortly thereafter Dr. Harry Yarrow arrived with the U. S. Army Engineer Corps, who were doing a geographical survey west of the 100th meridian. Schumacher and Yarrow agreed to divide their efforts, and the territory. Yarrow started digging on the mainland and Schumacher undertook to investigate the Santa Barbara Channel Islands. The third party—considered interlopers by Schumacher, were a French scientific expedition financed by Alphonse Pinart, but undertaken by Léon de Cessac, a scientist known for his studies in physiography and volcanic phenomena (Grant 1965:25).

The stakes were high. Personal reputations rested on the ability to find and control certain sites and the digging paid off handsomely. The Yarrow party, for example, removed as much as fifteen tons of artifacts from mainland sites.

These, and many others, including amateurs, sightseers and developers, set the shovels digging and the dirt flying all over the Los Angeles Basin. Unfortunately not many of these people had the slightest scientific training, or concern for the sites they were pillaging. Hence much of what might have been learned was lost. Anthropology, of course was not an accepted science until the 1890's, but this cannot justify the wanton destruction of so many sites.

Schumacher provided stiff competition for Léon de Cessac, who had set up operation on Santa Cruz Island, then under control of a French wool company. First, he told de Cessac that it was against the law to remove archaeological objects from the continental United States to a foreign country, and he got local authorities to back him up, threatening to confiscate any artifact collections. Then, he used his influence to persuade the Secretary of the Smithsonian Institution to have Congress pass an act forbidding the exportation of prehistoric objects. The Secretary eventually declined to approach the Senate, and the matter was closed.

Ignoring all threats, de Cessac continued digging. His operations had barely started again, when his patron Alphonse Pinart informed him that the inheritance which had funded the expedition was gone, and that he would be unable to finance further excavations. De Cessac took this news in stride, and continued work for nearly a year, until his own resources of mainly borrowed funds, dried up. In that time he amassed a stunning collection of over three thousand artifacts, now in the Musée de l'Homme in Paris. The highlights of his collection include some wooden bowls from Chumash territory, similar to those used by the Gabrielino. He also excavated a remarkable collection of Gabrielino steatite effigies that resemble sea birds (Reichlen & Heizer:1963).

Gabrielino woman. Note basket worn on head and European dress. Courtesy Southwest Museum.

LONE WOMAN

THE 1830'S WERE A TIME of transition for the Gabrielino: the mission system began to fail; most of the native population had been subjugated, or brought into the Christian realm; fewer and fewer traditional village sites existed, or were even in use; and most disturbing of all, the Gabrielino lifeways became a distant memory for many. The Mission fathers still saw their life's work ahead of them, and set in motion a plan to round up all the remaining Gabrielino and Chumash of the offshore Islands. Apparently, they believed it would be a sin to leave the unbaptized to their own devices.

Thus in 1835, a delapidated supply ship named *Peor es nada* ("Worse than nothing") went to San Nicolàs Island to find any remaining Gabrielino. The Islands had previously been difficult for the mission fathers to reach, and it was well-known that the Island population had incurred many hardships, not the least of which was their slaughter, by Russian whalers with a Kodiak Indian crew, in the 1820's. Still some natives were able to continue living in the traditional manner, by virtue of their distance from San Gabriel and other coastal missions.

Peor es nada set sail from San Pedro Bay on a mission of *white man's* mercy. On board the mountain man Bill Williams, who had come west with the Walker Expedition two years before.

Williams was accustomed to rough travel, and he had his own reasons for going to San Nicolàs Island. He wanted an Indian wife from among those rounded up.

Of all the Islands in Gabrielino territory, San Nicolàs is the furthest out from shore and the least hospitable. There is little shelter, and nothing in the way of a good harbor, though a sand spit forms one end. The island itself rises to a gentle plateau, but everywhere the surf is heavy. It suffers the brunt of Pacific storms, and its sandy shores are constantly swept by high wind and rough seas. It was a formidable retreat, which at this time was home to a small band of Indians. The crew of the *Peor es nada* dropped anchor outside the surf line and set about their task. In all, eighteen Indians were rounded up, brought to the beach and made ready for embarking. The wind swept sand into the air while the blue California sky began to pale and go crimson at the horizon. The Indians stood by with their meager belongings while the boat was made ready. Suddenly, one distressed young woman made signs that she had left her child behind, and wanted to go back for it. She was last seen moving away from shore, alone, climbing a sand dune in search of her child.

Soon, the wind that often plagues the island became stronger. The Captain, fearing that the high seas would capsize his poorly-made boat, waited no longer and hurried the remaining Indians aboard. With some reluctance he set sail, leaving the woman. The Captain spoke of his intention of returning for her. But fate had taken a hand in her destiny, as the *Peor es nada* drifted away over the blue horizon.

The Indians were put ashore at San Pedro where they were split into two groups with some being sent to Los Angeles, while the others were taken to San Gabriel Mission.

Informed of the missing woman's plight, the Padres deliberated on her fate, always meaning to *rescue* her. But no rescue was forthcoming, and her fate was sealed when the *Peor es nada* sank on a trip to San Francisco hauling lumber. This sorry schooner was the only boat of size then plying the coast. Gone were the days when the Gabrielino would venture out onto the open sea in their rough-hewn plank canoes.

Fifteen years passed as easily as sand washes along the surf line. On San Nicolàs Island, old village sites were covered with drifting sand dunes, or overgrown with bunch grass. The young woman's story was told in rumor and was forgotten. Everyone believed she was dead. For a decade-and-a-half, no one looked for her.

In 1850, a cursory search was conducted for the "lost woman" by a passing ship but no one was found.

Then in the spring of 1852, George Nidever, who had also come west with the Walker Expedition went to hunt seagull eggs on the Islands. These eggs were a sought after delicacy in Santa Barbara. He took with him a crew of Chumash Indians who were adept at hunting otters, and finding eggs.

The fierce wind off San Nicolàs Island lived up to its reputation, but although the crew found no eggs, they did find however something more interesting—signs of human habitation!

There were fresh footprints near a makeshift camp, several hundred yards inland from shore. Nidever and his crew discovered three circular enclosures (he called them "windbreaks") about six or seven feet in diameter, positioned on a small dune plateau. They searched that day until forced to stop by a storm that drove them to shelter for almost a week. When it lifted, Nidever headed his battered boat and crew straight for Santa Barbara.

Nine months later, in the winter of 1852-53, Nidever made another trip to San Nicolàs to hunt sea otter. The large kelp beds surrounding the Island would provide good hunting, he was sure. There was another reason for the trip, too. Father Gonzales had pressed him to make a thorough search of the island for the *lost woman*. Apparently, Father Gonzales had been trying for years to get someone to search the island with little luck.

On landing, they saw "fresh footprints." Carl Dittman, in his report of this trip, says that they also found a basket covered by a seal skin, containing, tanned bird skins, abalone fishhooks and sewing equipment. There was also a rope about eight meters in length. Dittman reports: *This sinew rope was twisted as evenly as the best rope I have ever seen. I think that it was used in snaring seals, by making a noose and spreading it on the rocks near the beach where the seals were accustomed to sleep* (Heizer & Elsasser 1961:6). Here was clear evidence of someone on the island. Nidever thought they should leave the contents of the basket strewn on the ground to see if anyone would replace them. They spent the next several days hunting otter. On the fourth day, a gale started and increased, so they were forced to decamp to San Miguel Island for protection. The bad weather continued and soon they returned to Santa Barbara, without making contact with the mysterious island woman.

It was on the third trip, in June 1853, that they finally found the *Lone Woman* as she has been called. Nidever had made preparations to stay on the island for several months during a time of good weather. Once again, when they came ashore they found footprints and this time were able to locate a trail which they followed until they came across a woman. Here is how Carl Dittman describes that day:

I began to look about me and finally discovered at a distance on the northeast side of the ridge and about halfway up to its top, a small black object that from where I stood looked like a crow seated on a bush. I saw it move and so went towards it. I soon discovered it was an Indian woman...While I was still some distance away two dogs, probably the same we had seen the day before, began to growl, whereupon she gave a yell and they went away.

Dittman signaled to George Nidever and the rest of the crew to approach. She was not afraid of them, and even spoke to the Nidever's Chumash crewmen, but they could not understand her. She was spoken to in several different dialects, but could not understand what was said to her.

When they first approached her, she was sitting near a hut made from whale rib bones and sage brush. She had been stripping blubber from a piece of seal skin. To Nidever's surprise, she greeted them with *dignity and politeness bowing and smiling with ease and self possession* (Heizer & Elsasser 1961:42). The woman was voluble, talking at length to herself, or to them but, alas, no one could fathom what she said. They soon found that they could communicate by hand signs and facial expression. She offered them wild onions that she had been roasting in a small fire.

Around her hut were the pieces of her life—a few baskets, some half finished, a long rope for catching seals, fishing lines of sinew. The blubber she had been preparing was skewered by stakes and set out to dry on sinew lines. On the ground nearby lay fish hooks and bone sewing needles.

Water basket thought to have been made by the "Lone Woman."

She appeared to Nidever to be about fifty years of age but still strong and quite active. She was not dark skinned and her hair was matted and while probably originally black, had at length been bleached reddish-brown by the sun. Her only clothing was a dress made of cormorant skins. It was fitted close to the neck and sleeveless. Nidever reports that she had another of these dresses in a basket near by. There was no evidence of a child, who would be eighteen or more years of age.

In the ensuing days, the hunters did their work, making camp in the middle of the island. They hunted sea otter for about a month. The woman helped by bringing them fresh water and fire wood. A crew member made her a dress, which she liked very much.

Nidever conveyed to her that they meant to take her off the island when their hunting was done. He reports that they gained her confidence by treating her with kindness, and by assuring her that her belongings would be preserved and brought along in the boat. At first she did not understand, but Carl Dittman went through the motions of leaving by packing some of her things, where upon she realized what was meant. She apparently accepted this idea, and set about packing her possessions which were transported aboard the boat. When the hunting was finished, they all broke camp and returned to Santa Barbara.

For the most part, while they were on the island, the weather had proven gentle but on the trip home a gale blew up buffeting them about the Channel waters. The Indian woman made motions that she intended to stop the storm by offering a prayer and did so throughout the day until the storm ceased. She seemed satisfied that she had done her work.

On arriving at Santa Barbara, she was very excited at seeing an ox pulling a cart, speaking and laughing gaily. Moments later, George Nidever's son rode up on a horse which delighted her even more.

News spread fast of the arrival of the woman and she was visited by many in the town and quite a few people from afar.

She was apparently very happy and liked to eat sweets, fruit and vegetables. She was given gifts of trinkets and money, but she saw no value in them except for the pleasure of dividing them among the Nidever children (Heizer & Elsasser 1961:11). She danced and sang for her company and told them about her life in gestures. The Padres made some effort to find someone who could communicate verbally with her and sent for various Indians from the district. But this was the land of the Chumash, and no Gabrielino Indians were sent for, so no one was ever found with whom she could speak. Several of her words were recorded: *to-co* meaning hide; *te-gua*, the sky; *na-che*, a man; and *pinche*, the body. No one thought to record more, or perhaps her words are lost to us. It was on the basis of these four words that A. L. Kroeber believed the *Lone Woman* and her tribe spoke the Shoshonean dialect of the Gabrielino (Grant 1965:132).

She said by signs that in the beginning when left alone on the island she wandered for days without food or water and slept very little. Her clothes became torn and her feet bloody. She never found her child. Some reports suggest that it was eaten by wild dogs. It was a dark time for her but out of it grew the will to survive.

She told the Nidevers that she had once been very sick but recovered to good health. On occasion, she had seen boats pass by her island, but they had never stopped.

The *Lone Woman* stayed with George Nidever and his wife for a little less than two months when the sudden change in diet, or possibly disease, took its toll and she fell ill. Efforts were made to nurse her. She was brought seal blubber which she had eaten on the island. It was prepared by roasting in the manner that she had done for most of her life, but she would not eat it. In a short time, a mere seven weeks from her first setting foot on the mainland, she died. On her deathbed she had been baptized Juana Maria by the mission priests, one of the last victims of a system that had sought to be the benefactor of the California Indians, but which in reality was their doom. Her clothes and possessions were taken by Father Gonzales and reportedly sent to Rome. They have never been found (Heizer & Elsasser, 1961).

Presumed Lone Woman of San Nicolàs Island. From a glass negative by Hayward & Muzzell of Santa Barbara found with one of Mrs. George Nidever. Courtesy Southwest Museum..

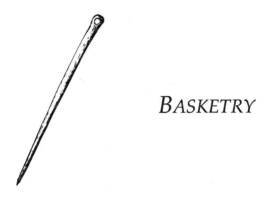

BASKETRY

THE EXTANT BASKETS OF the Gabrielino are few, but those that do exist show clearly that the Gabrielino were superb basket makers. So beautifully wrought were these baskets that the Spanish explorers and settlers avidly collected them for their own use. There are several historical accounts which attest to the variety and intricacy of Gabrielino basketry and to the many uses the Indians made of them. Father Pedro Font, one chronicler of the Anza expedition, wrote in his diary that there was barter and trade for baskets in nearly every village encountered.

Baskets were indispensable in the daily life of the Gabrielino. They were used in every activity, from food collecting and preparation, to carrying and storing water. Baskets were used as plates and bowls, for serving, as seed beaters, for straining, leaching, cooking and storing food, for carrying large burdens, for fishing, for gambling, for storing small trinkets and precious ritual objects, for use in the rituals themselves and in historical times as presentation gifts to important persons.

The basket weavers used two basic methods—coiling and twining. The coiled ware included baskets for food preparation and seed storage, trays, bucket and basin shaped baskets, burden and trinket baskets and women's basketry hats. The twined ware was used for fishing, seed beating and straining, leaching and water storage.

The Gabrielino lived in a relatively dry climate, although there is some evidence that as recently as eight hundred years ago, Southern California was wetter than at present. The Inland and Island Gabrielino probably had moderate water supplies. Presented with this need to transport and store this vital resource, they developed an ingenious method for making watertight baskets. Many baskets, especially twined baskets, were extremely fine and so tightly woven that they held water on their own even though they weren't meant for liquid storage. To solve the problem of long-term water storage, the Gabrielino would line the inside of a basket with asphaltum (tar that seeped from underground deposits). These water-storage baskets could be the size of a small water bottle, or quite large, holding five or six gallons. They were twined from rush or tule, were rougher in appearance than most coiled ware and generally very plain, with little or no decoration.

George Nidever, a fur trapper, recorded the process of lining a water storage basket with asphaltum that he witnessed on San Nicolàs Island. He speaks of the *Lone Woman*:

She had built a fire and had several small stones about the size of a walnut heating in it. Taking one of the vessels, which was in the shape and size very like a demi-john, except that the neck and mouth were much longer, she dropped a few pieces of asphaltum within it and as soon as the stones were well heated they were dropped in on top of the asphaltum. They soon melted it, when resting on the bottom of the vessel on the ground, she gave it a rotary motion with both hands until the interior was completely covered with asphaltum. These vessels hold water well, and if kept full may be placed with safety in a hot sun (Nidever 1973:14).

For storage of dry materials—seeds, acorns and such, the Gabrielino made large coiled baskets that were kept indoors. These storage baskets were sometimes covered with another basket and weighted with a stone. These plainly designed juncus basket graneries were purely utilitarian although sometimes ceremonial regalia was stored in them.

Basketry bowls were used for serving food and for standard measures of seeds offered in trade. They are coiled, fairly large, and somewhat shallow. Basket dishes were held in the palm of the hand and used for serving individual portions. They are similar in design and shape to the basket bowls but smaller in size.

The Gabrielino made many kinds of trays—small and large coiled winnowers and basket trays for serving. The same tray may have had multiple purposes, being used for serving food and later for gambling.

Basket hopper mortar. Courtesy Southwest Museum.

The basket hopper mortar is an example of the often ingenious use the Gabrielino made of their basketry. A coiled, bottomless basket, perhaps one that the bottom had worn out of was affixed with asphaltum to a stone or wooden mortar and in this fashion the seeds or vegetables being pulverized were contained on the grinding surface.

Some of the most beautiful baskets the Gabrielino made were not for food uses but for storing small ritual objects, shell-bead money and jewelry. These were the wonderfully-made globular and bottleneck trinket baskets. These small, highly decorated coiled baskets were ellipsoidal in shape with a narrow opening.

The Gabrielino used a variety of basketry materials, most of which were found locally. Willow was cut in the wet areas near the rivers and natural springs. Rush, cattail, and tule were harvested in the esteros and small ponds. They were spread on the bank and left to dry and then separated and bundled for later use. Grass (*Epicampes regins*), was gathered in the summer.

Bundles of rush (*Juncus balticus*), or deer grass (*Muhlenbergia rigens*), were used for coil foundations. For the wrapping and design, split *Juncus* was common, giving the basket a natural straw or tan color, or even black. The Gabrielino used three *Juncus* color patterns—red, green, and black. Split peeled sumac root (*rhus trilobata*), was used for for the foundations, or for the stitching. Of all these materials *Juncus* was by far the most prevalent. (Ebeling, 1986).

Gabrielino basketry designs are sometimes quite complex, though primarily geometric. The principle characteristics of these beautiful pieces are that they had bundled coils, and in stitching, the awl enters from the inside of the basket (Harrington 1942). Gabrielino baskets are started with two pairs of four-warp elements and the coiling moves from left to right, this being typical of all Southern California tribes. The Gabrielino also used some realistic designs in their baskets (Dawson and Deetz 1965) (Turnbaugh 1986:200).

It is thought that the Gabrielino had a very explicit system of rules and design standards governing basket making. Probably every type of basket and every design element had some meaning that has now been lost to us. This was true of other tribes in California and elsewhere. Throughout California, basket making was a high point of material culture. The Gabrielino were no exception.

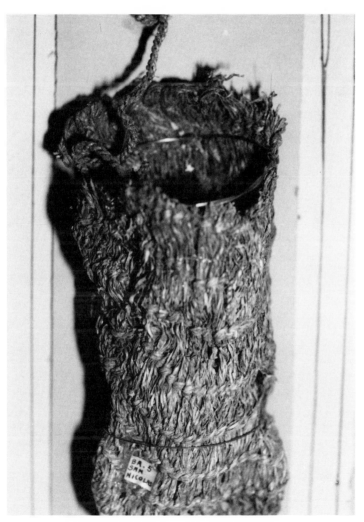

Woven fiber bag or purse from San Nicolàs Island.
Courtesy Antelope Valley Indian Museum.

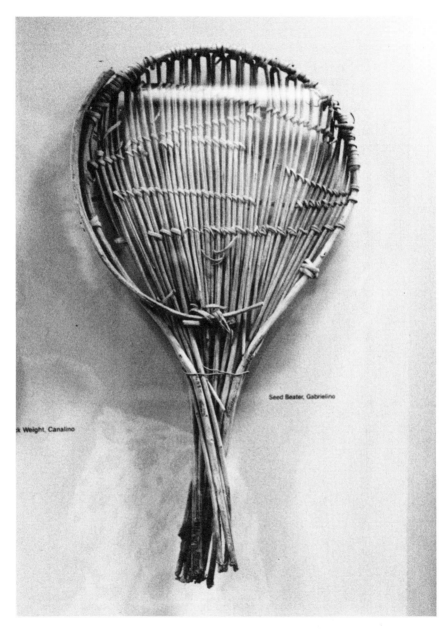

Wicker seed beater. Photograph by Bruce W. Miller. Courtesy Southwest Museum.

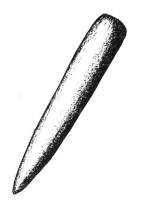

WOOD & STONE TOOLS

THE WOODEN OBJECTS and dishes the Gabrielino made are quite extraordinary. They are handworked, smeared with red ochre, and polished to a lustrous sheen. The best of them have a fineness and definition that has few parallels even in our own day. Unfortunately very few of them survive today.

There are some historical accounts of finely-made wooden bowls and other objects. Costansó, the engineer with the Portolá expedition noted: *The men make beautiful bowls of wood with solid inlays of shell or bone, and some vessels of great capacity, contracted at the mouth, which appear as if turned in a lathe, in fact, with this machine they could not be turned out better hollowed or more perfectly formed (Hemert-Engert and Teggart 1910:45).*

Other wooden implements and utensils included ladles, spoons, dishes, trays, cups, lifting sticks and mashing paddles. These functional wooden items were made of ash, willow, toyon, redwood, and cottonwood as suited the craftsperson's needs and resources.

The Gabrielino followed three basic steps in making a wooden bowl. First came the selection of the wood, then shaping and hollowing, and finally the decorating and polishing. The wood was worked into the desired shape and then hollowed. They may have been shaped by controlled burning of excess wood and then grinding away the charcoal. Then the wooden bowl or jar would be dry polished and a mixture of animal fat and red ochre was smeared inside and out to seal the wood. Finally, the bowl was left to dry in the sun. After drying, the bowl was polished again to a fine sheen (Hudson & Blackburn 1981:248).

For the centuries that the Gabrielino occupied the California coast, various kinds of stone implements were used. Over the years, the style and shape of these tools changed. They would even vary from village to village, depending on the rock material available for use. Sandstone, which was quite commonly available, was the rock of choice for making metates, manos, mortars, bowls and pestles. Basaltic rock and granite were also used, though less frequently. Bedrock mortars were made on a sandstone shelf or outcroppings.

Light-gray steatite came from Catalina Island, where it was mined in numerous quarries. It was used for cooking pots and other implements that would be subject to heat. It was from hard steatite (serpentine), that they made their most beautiful objects— charmstones, pipes, ritual bowls, effigies and ornaments. Knives, scrapers, drills, and projectile points were made from chert, jasper, chalcedony, and obsidian. Obsidian was obtained in trade-sized chunks from the Southwestern and Sierra tribes.

There is evidence that steatite, or soapstone as it is more commonly called was mined on Catalina Island as far back as four thousand years. These mining activities increased sharply seven hundred years ago, as the Southern California trading economy heated up (Wlodarski 1979:331).

Mortars used by the Indians to pulverize vegetal food, seeds and occasionally meat were made by chipping away a large, round piece of sandstone. A pestle, usually made of sandstone, was the grinding implement that accompanied the mortar.

Four steps in the process of making a mortar.
A. A suitable round piece of sandstone is selected.
A stone chisel and hand held hammerstone are used
to peck a groove around the top edge of the mortar.
B. Knobs of sandstone are pecked in the top
and then lopped off with a strong blow.
C. The rim is formed and the final contour
of the outer edge is started.
D. To finish, the bowl of the mortar
is pecked out. (Bryan 1961).

Small sandstone mortar and pestle. Photograph by Bruce W. Miller Courtesy Antelope Valley Indian Museum.

Another important stone implement was the anvil, a small, round rock with a slight divot, where the acorn was placed before striking. The hammer was in turn, a small round, hand held rock. The Gabrielino also had curious round stones with holes in the center shaped vaguely like a donut. These have proven to be weights for digging sticks, although they may also have been used for war clubs and fishing weights. Some of these objects are polished and decorated with incised designs and may have been used for ritual purposes, such as the head of a sunstaff used in winter solstice ceremonies. Comals, introduced by the Spanish during mission times were flat, rectangular, slightly concave stones, with a hole at one end so they could by taken from the fire with a hooked stick. These were used like frying pans.

Steatite Cup. Courtesy Antelope Valley Indian Museum.

Sandstone Cup. Courtesy Antelope Valley Indian Museum.

Steatite paint mortar and pestle, 2" diameter. Courtesy Antelope Valley Indian Museum.

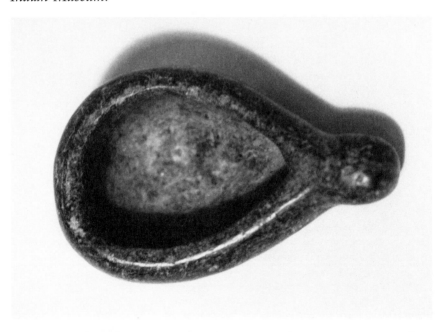

Small serpentine finger bowl possibly for ritual use. Courtesy Antelope Valley Indian Museum.

EFFIGIES

GABRIELINO EFFIGIES are largely zoomorphic in form, consisting mainly of marine mammals and water birds, although canoes and pendants were also made. They were used as a kind of personal talisman. Effigies were fashioned of stone, mainly steatite because of its relatively soft nature and its ability to take a good finish. Sandstone, serpentine, wood, and bone were also used in some areas.

Effigies made from steatite often have a high, black gloss probably obtained by first greasing and then smoking the surface, before polishing. These effigies have both a ritual and economic significance for the Gabrielino with particular effigies possibly having specific meanings. They are thought to have been considered power objects that allowed the owner access to the magic and spirits of this world.

In the boys' initiation ceremony, a boy would be touched on the back of the neck with the shaman's effigy conferring strength. Other types of objects were also sacred, such as shaman's pipes and ceremonial paint mortars. Some shamans wore a small board which was painted red and adorned with snake rattles (Johnson:1962,71).

59

Seatite killer whale effigy found on the Rindle Estate, Los Angeles County. Courtesy Southwest Museum.

Effigies can be divided into two stylistic categories for identification purposes: realistic and abstract. The realistic figurines often have natural attributes, such as drilled eyes, blowholes, mouth incisions, and dorsal fins. Effigies also often have decorative incising, or shell bead inlay (Hoover 1974:34). A large group of pelican stones found by de Cessac in 1877-1879, on San Nicolàs Island, are primarily abstract representations and have no incising or shell-bead inlay. Some of them have bird-like markings that represent wings and other avian anatomy.

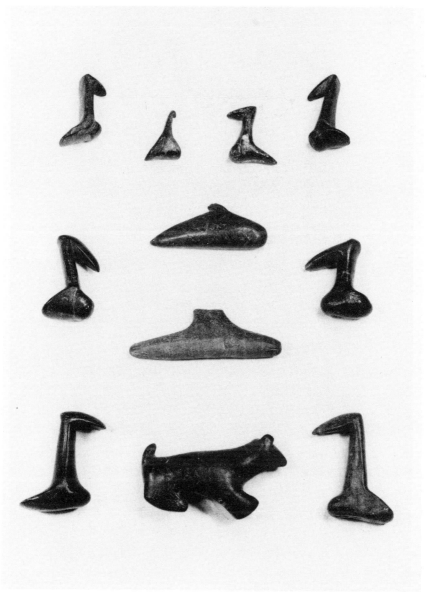

Seatite charms from Catalina Island and other sites. Courtesy Southwest Museum.

Swordfish effigy. Photograph Bruce W. Miller. Courtesy Los Angeles County Natural History Museum.

Steatite Charms and fetishes from Southern California. Courtesy Southwest Museum.

HUNTING

THE GABRIELINO WERE practical hunters. While they did not farm or make use of advanced agricultural methods until the Spanish came, they did have skilled hunters. Hunting added to their highly developed gathering activity, gave them a large and varied subsistence base.

For hunting, they used bows and arrows, javelins, curved throwing sticks, clubs, slings, various snares, deadfall traps and all the wiles of a people close to nature. They were, by all accounts expert marksmen.

Hinged-stick snare. These snares were placed on the ground and attached to a bowed tree limb. A wooden trigger (not seen here) would trip the tree limb and force the two jaw-like sticks together.

Some taboos surrounded the hunt. Men did not have sex with their wives before the hunt for fear of bad luck. There was also a proscription on eating during the time of the hunt or of eating from any animal the hunter himself had killed. The same was said to be true of fisherman (Johnson: 1962,34). Boscana mentions that when boys went out to hunt rabbits or ground squirrels, they would go in pairs so as to swap game and be able to eat. If the taboo against eating was broken the hunter would sicken *and start feeling pains in his body and start wasting away, getting thin like a hectic person* (Harrington 1934,46).

Two types of bow were used: the self bow for small game; and the sinew-backed bow for fighting, and for larger animals such as deer. The self bow was an unadorned staff of wood about three and a half feet, or less, in length. They were fashioned out of durable yet pliable wood. Probably elderberry, juniper, or nascent oak. Self bows were kept unstrung until they were ready to shoot and were favored because they could be easily strung. Bowstring was made of two or three-ply woven vegetal fiber (probably milkweed and or dogbane) or from deer sinew.

Sinew-backed bows were under four feet in length, made of toyon or elder and had pin type nocks. The best, sinew-backed bows were fashioned with the use of hot water, unlike lesser bows that were shaped by heating the bow staff in fire. Sinew backed bows were always made in recurved style. To attach the sinew, animal skin glue was smeared evenly on the bow staff, the sinew was laid on in strips, then more sinew was wrapped radially, to greatly increase the strength of the wood. Bows and arrows were sometimes painted red with iron oxide that was greatly favored by Southern California natives.

Arrows were of several types. The self arrow was a shaft of straightened wood with feather fletching, V-shaped nocks and fire hardened points. These arrows were made of hard wood and were used for hunting small game, or for sporting competition.

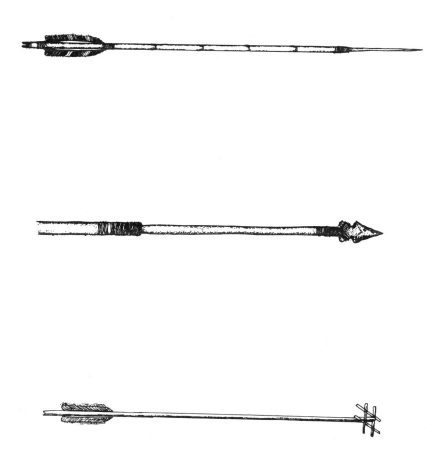

Wooden tipped composite arrow. (above) Stone tipped composite arrow. (middle) A chert point is lashed to the wooden foreshaft with sinew and asphaltum.   Cruciform arrow for hunting birds (below).

Composite arrows were the most elaborate and the longest of the arrows the Gabrielino used. With sinew wrapping, radial fletching and painted or pyrographic decorations, these arrows were things of terrible beauty, deadly and wonderful in the making. Carrizo cane was cut and allowed to dry completely, then straightened by a heated, grooved straightening stone. When straight, a firesharpened hardwood shaft was attached with sinew to one end by inserting it into the hollow cane. On the other end a hardwood nock was inserted and attached with sinew. On a stone-tipped, composite arrow, a chert point would be attached to the hardwood foreshaft before it was inserted into the cane mainshaft. Hafting the chert point to the hardwood shaft was done with very fine sinew. Fletching was attached with sinew wrapping and trimmed with a hot coal to the desired shape (Hudson 1974).

Pronghorn (Antilocarpa americana). Often mistake for deer these small antelopes were a common site in early California.

Gabrielino hunters used decoy headdresses to approach their prey without startling it. Deer and antelope headdresses were commonly used to good advantage. Costansó, with the Portolá expedition of 1796, commented on this Southern California technique:

In killing deer and antelopes, they employ an admirable device. They preserve the skin of the head and part of the neck of one of these animals...This mask they put like a cap on the head. On seeing a deer or antelope, they crawl slowly with the left hand on the ground, carrying the bow and four arrows in the right. They lower and raise their head, turning it from one side to the other, and make the other movements so characteristic of these animals, that they attract them without difficulty to the decoy, and having them at short range, they discharge their arrows with sure effect (Hemert-Engert and Teggart 1910:49).

It is believed that the Gabrielino used arrow poisons (usually rattlesnake), but the efficacy of these organic poisons has not been determined. Slings were also used for killing birds and small game. Seals and sea lions were hunted with clubs and spears.

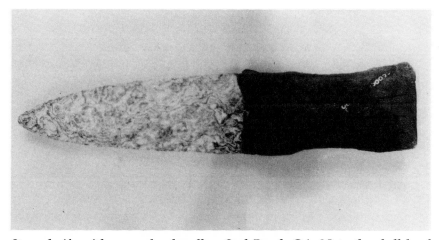

Stone knife with a wooden handle—Seal Beach CA. Note the shell bead inlay on handle. Courtesy Southwest Museum.

Chert and obsidian arrowpoints from Malaga Cove, the site of a University of Southern California archaeological dig in 1936. This was the site of the prominent Gabrielino village Chowigna, dating from before Cabrillo's 1542 landing.

FISHING

THE GABRIELINO BUILT three types of watercraft, the plank canoe, called *ti'at*, the dugout and the tule balsa canoe. For fishing gear they had harpoons, fishspears, hook, line, and sinker, fishnets and bone gorges. With this gear and their sea-going craft they sought fish, seals, sea otters, shark and even sea birds. They fished along the shore and on the open ocean, taking advantage of the tides and the relatively calm seas around the Channel Islands and San Pedro Bay. The annual runs of albacore, yellow and blue fin tuna and some of the smaller pelagic fishes such as sardines, were all sought after. In the winter months they relied more on easily-obtained shellfish (some of the best low tides occur in winter), or dried fish caught in the fair-weather months. It is likely that some of the large coastal population moved inland seasonaly, thus reducing the subsistence needs in the coast villages.

What freshwater fishing for trout and other species that was done was minimal and done when the opportunity presented itself. Such anadromous fish were readily caught with fishspears and weir nets in dammed up pools.

CANOES

The plank canoe which was unique in North America was made only by the Gabrielino and their Chumash neighbors. It was this craft which allowed them to travel to the islands and to take the abundant schools of pelagic fish that visited the Southern California coast. This canoe impressed most of the early explorers who saw it. Today, it is considered the Gabrielino's finest technological achievement. Font gave an excellent description of the Chumash plank canoe similar to that built by the Gabrielino.

They are very carefully made of several planks which they work with no other tools but their shells and flints. They join them at the seams by sewing them with very strong thread which they have and fit the joints with pitch...Some of the launches are decorated with little shells and all are painted red with hematite. In shape they are like a little boat without ribs, ending in two points...In the middle there is a somewhat elevated plank laid across from side to side to serve as a seat and to preserve the convexity of the frame...They carry some poles about six feet in length which end in blades these being the oars with which they row alternately on one side and then on the other (Bolton 1930:252).

The plank canoe was frameless, with no internal, structural ribs and was made from driftwood, mainly redwood, or from pine that grew in the San Gabriel Mountains. Redwood from Northern California would float down the coast after a storm and land on the Southern California beaches. There it was collected and brought to the villages to dry. Redwood is relatively light and has the essential qualities of being easily worked and of being durable.

Wood for canoe making was very carefully selected for a straight grain and no knots. Knots would dry out and crack, causing the boat to leak. The best wood available was used for the bottom plank and the first row around the hull. Larger pieces of wood were split with a whale bone wedge, or deer antler and then shaped, trimmed and leveled with adzes and a chert knife. The usual adze had a blade made from a sharpened Pismo clam or chert. After the planks were split, those selected for hull boards were beveled and finished with sharkskin sandpaper. Caulking was a mixture of heated tar and pine pitch.

Holes were bored in the hull planks using hand drills tipped with chert, or bone. The planks were then laid edge to edge and lashed together with vegetal fiber string. The fiber was wrapped several times through the holes to tie the planks together giving the hull additional strength. Once fitted and lashed, caulking tule (the heart of dry tule rush) was forced into the cracks on the outside of the hull. The hull was then coated again with caulking tar.

Next, the structural crossplank was added at midship to reinforce the craft. Finally, splashboards were attached to the gunwales, stern and prow.

With the structural elements completed the plank canoe was sanded and painted with red ochre and coated with a sealant greatly enhancing the integrity of the boat.

Plank canoes were both fast and light and varied in length from ten to thirty feet. The canoe was propelled with a double-bladed paddle. There was no anchor although the canoe was sometimes held in place, when at sea, by pulling kelp over the side to keep it from drifting. Otherwise, the fishermen would just drift with the current as they fished. While fairly seaworthy, these plank canoes did leak and so a boy would be brought along to bail water.

The tule balsa canoe was used by the Gabrielino in lagoons and at sea. It was quickly built—start to finish, from the cutting of the tule to the launching, took as little as three days.

To make the tule canoe, green bulrush (*Scirpus acutus*) was cut and then spread out to dry. After a few days, when the tule was partially dried, it was taken up and formed into bundles, the length of which depended on the size of the boat to be made. A willow pole ran the length of each bundle, to add strength to the body of the canoe. Bundles were tied together at the stern and prow, to form a raised point and then tied to the bottom bundle along their length. There was no seat in the balsa canoe. Finally, the outside of the canoe was coated with tar to add bouyancy and prevent rot (Hudson, Timbrook, Rempe 1978:27-31).

The tule canoe was bulky, but lightweight and easily carried overhead. When cared for properly, these canoes were both versatile and durable. It is said that the Gabrielino could even make a fire on board these craft to attract and cook fish. They did this by coating the interior of the canoe with a hardened mud on which the fire was started. Water was always handy, so there was little chance of a fire getting out of control.

Tule canoes were also furnished with a double-bladed paddle for propulsion, or were paddled with the arms when lying in the prone position. They were mainly used for near-shore fishing in natural harbors and bays, but occasionally they were used for trips to the islands.

Chumash canoe paddle blade collected by Vancouver in 1793. Note the repair made with fiber cord. Courtesy the British Museum.

FISHING

The Gabrielino employed all the standard methods of gathering from sea and stream. They used a great variety of fishing tackle and nets. Netting was knotted fiber made from sea grass or dogbane. Both men and women worked on cordage and the Gabrielino spent a lot of time making and repairing these nets. Fishing, like hunting was considered a male activity. Nets were large and deployed in a circular fashion from a canoe. The net enclosure then snagged any fish that happened by and was especially effective for large fish, whose gills were caught in the netting.

The Gabrielino fished in the sea and at the surf line, with hook, line and sinker. Hooks were made of shell, wood and bone. The circular fish hook was common and usually made from abalone shell. Occasionally, bone or mussel shell would subsitute. Common bait for fishing was shellfish (mussels and clams), or fish. Bone gorges are the simplest of all hooks, merely a straight bipointed piece of bone that is attached at the center to a line. The hook is dangled in the water until a fish is attracted and takes a bite. A quick jerk lodges the unbaited hook crossways in the fish's mouth.

Conical wicker fish trap. After being submerged in place at the opening in a fish weir, fish were driven down steam into the trap (Hudson and Blackburn 1982:149).

Unfinished abalone shell fishhook. This circular fishhook slug is in the final stage of manufacture. Courtesy Antelope Valley Indian Museum.

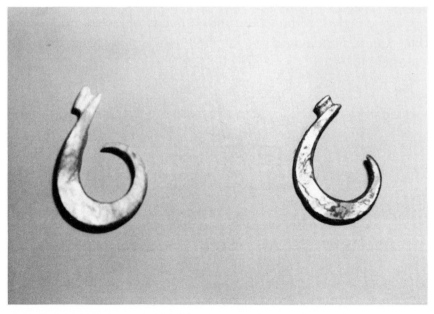

Two finished abalone shell fishhooks. Antelope Valley Indian Museum.

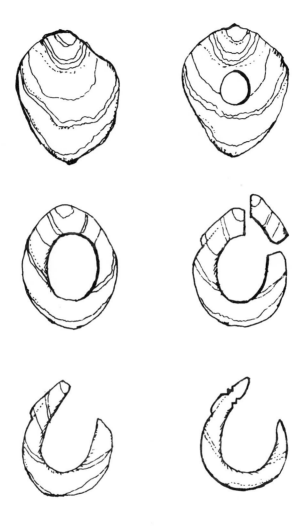

How a circular fishhook is made. A circular piece of shell, usually abalone (Haliotis), is broken off with a hammerstone. A chert or stone drill with the aid of an abrasive sand and water paste perforates the round piece of shell. The hole is widened by grinding and the outside is smoothed and rounded by rubbing on a stone slab. The tip of the hook and the shank are separated by removing a piece of shell or further grinding. The point of the shell hook is smoothed and sharpened and notches are made in the shank to attach the fiber string.

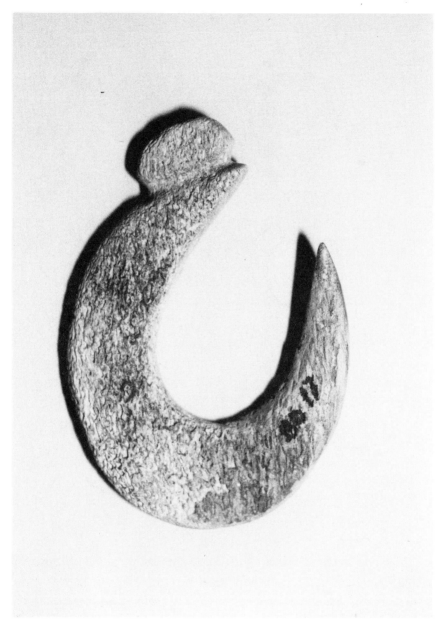

Large fishhook. This may have been used on large ocean going fishes. It also may have served as a meat hook or as a ceremonial object. Courtesy Antelope Valley Indian Museum.

FOOD

THE GABRIELINO GATHERED a wide range of wild foods, fished the streams and ocean, and hunted game. Their diet was broadly based and included most of the good sources of protein in their area. Their primary source of carbohydrates was from acorns. It is believed that as much as half their diet consisted of this staple.

Acorns were prepared by first removing the outer shell. The acorn cap was discarded, the nut was placed on a flat stone and then tapped with any handy, oval stone, or mano. The nut meats were extracted from the hull by an antler or pointed bone tool. The nut meats were then dried for several days before being placed in a storage granary. To eat, the cured nuts were crushed in a mortar, until they were a rough flour. This acorn meal was then placed in a shallow, sand pit, lined with leaves and leached repeatedly by pouring cold and then hot water over it, until the bitter tannin was washed away. Once leached, the acorn meal could be stored until the following day.

Acorns were gathered by placing them in a net bag, or cone-shaped carrying basket that was supported by a strap around the forehead. Everyone joined in the acorn gathering (Johnson 1962: 34).

The population of a village might change, depending on the time of the year and the food being gathered. During the best few weeks of the year, when the oaks dropped their acorns, a large effort would be made to gather as much as possible, before moisture or rodent and avian competition reduced the yield. Temporary gathering camps would be set up in the hills to harvest the California black oak, which grew at slightly-higher elevation than the coast live oak. Along the mid coastal ranges the white oak also gave a fine yield. Toyon and Christmas berry were also gathered at these acorn sites.

In the summer and fall the coastal fishing was at its height. In the spring, cresses and new shoots of wild sage and other plants were gathered for eating. The agava and yucca were harvested now; in high summer prickly pear, yucca and manzanite berries.

Chia sage (Salvia columbariae). Common in dry open areas below 5000 feet. The seed was roasted for food and used for a refreshing drink.

The list of Gabrielino food items is varied. It includes:

Game
Fish and *shellfish*
Seaweeds
Jicamas—used on the islands and served to Vizcaino's men (Johnson:1962,105).
Wild oats—stripped by hands and then parched and mashed.
Blackberries which grew in the wet areas around the riverbeds, (Johnson,1962,33).
Elderberry
Chia (Sage seed)
Bitter current
Islay (Hollyleaf cherry),—harvested and dried for several days then leached and ground into mush, the pits were also sought after for the kernals inside.
Lemonadeberry—an aromatic evergreen shrub the berries of which made a refreshing drink.
Prickley pear
Vegetable chewing gum from *Indian milkweed*,
Soaproot—stripped and wrapped in leaves and roasted.
White fly sugar obtained from from the underside of grasses.
Yellow jacket larve—eaten as delicacies.
Caterpillars
Tule roots—the tender shoots and pollen were used as food.
Pine nuts
There were of course many other food items not mentioned here.

Steatite cooking bowl. Height 13 inches. Courtesy San Luis Obispo County Historical Museum.

Incised steatite bowl. Courtesy Southwest Museum.

CLOTHING

NUMEROUS, EARLY REFERENCES to the Gabrielino describe them as going about virtually naked. They lived in the relatively mild Southern California climate and clothing was not an absolute necessity. They also preferred bare feet, but occasionally wore sandals made from hide of yucca fiber. No doubt there were times in winter when clothing was needed.

Women usually wore skirts woven of tule or grass. Sometimes these petticoats were made of the inner bark of willow, sycamore or cottonwood trees, which was cut in strips and worked to a fine softness. Generally, men wore nothing except a belt that was really a bit of netting or fiber string, from which they could suspend tools and food. Small capes were made of deer skin; and sea otter skins were used for their fineness and warmth.

Men, especially shamans wore feathered net skirts. This type of ceremonial skirt was for ritual purposes and not worn as daily dress.

The Gabrielino made great use of body paints, usually red, or black and red mixed to a sooty brown. Body paints were both decorative and functional. They could denote social status and station and might be identified with a particular village. Women covered themselves with red ochre, to prevent sunburn, giving their upper bodies a glossy look. This liberal use of red-ochre paint also prevented wrinkles and chapping of the skin.

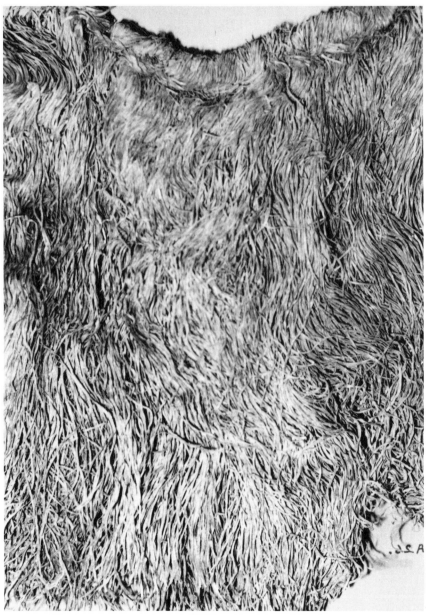

Woven grass skirt. Courtesy Antelope Valley Indian Museum.

Men wore their hair long and loose or braided and pinned up with the use of a bone hairpin and earrings of cane (Johnson, 1962:30). Women wore their hair long and usually loose.

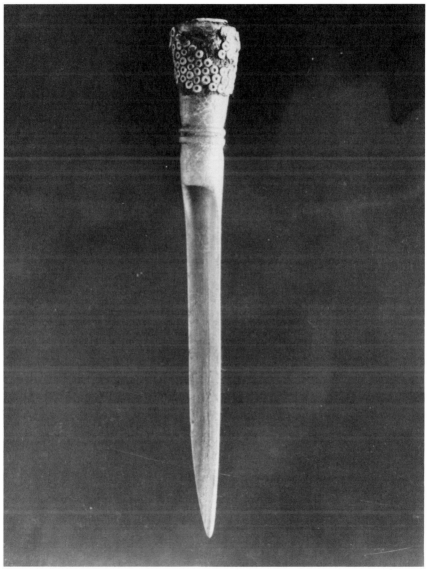

Bone awl or hair ornament. Decorated with olivella shell beads. Courtesy Southwest Museum.

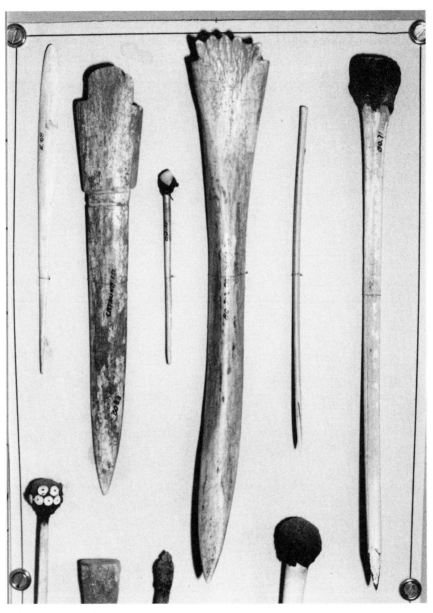

Carved bone hairpins. Note the black asphaltum tops for adherring decorative shell beads. Courtesy Antelope Valley Indian Museum.

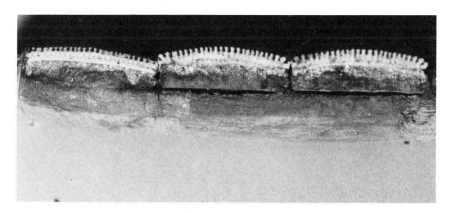

Unusual comb with a wooden base and baleen plate teeth. Courtesy Antelope Valley Indian Museum.

Tattooing was commonplace on both men and women. Young girls were often tattooed before puberty. Charcoal, or juice from deadly nightshade was rubbed into a small wound made with a cactus thorn to create an indelible tattoo.

Shell-bead necklaces were a favorite type of ornamentaion and were often worn in great numbers. Beads were made from red and black abalone, and from clam and olivella shells. Stone, and seed beads were also combined with shell beads as spacers and for variation in the design. These bead necklaces sometimes represented wealth.

Steatite finger rings. Courtesy Antelope Valley Indian Museum.

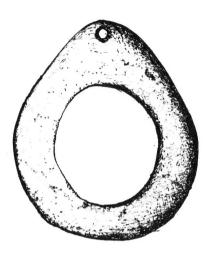

Steatite ornament. Courtesy Southwest Museum.

Perforated steatite tablets (pendants) from Catalina Museum. Photo courtesy Southwest Museum.

Incised sandstone pendant. Note that Gabrielino incising is primarily geometric in nature. Courtesy Antelope Valley Indian Museum.

Olivella shell bead necklace with a steatite pendant strung on rawhide. Courtesy Antelope Valley Indian Museum.

Olivella shell bead necklace with sandstone pendant. Photograph Bruce W. Miller. Courtesy Antelope Valley Indian Museum.

Shell artifacts from Catalina Island. Bracelet, sand dollar pendant, finger ring (small dark object laying on bracelet) and shell bead necklace. Courtesy Southwest Museum.

SHELTER

A TULE THATCHED HOUSE served as shelter for the Gabrielino. These structures were hemispherical, or conical in shape. Spanish explorers described them as having the shape of orange halves with a open smokehole for ventilation and light at the top, near the center. These circular huts were 15 to 50 feet in diameter and could house as few as one family or as many as thirty people. They were surprisingly large and roomy.

In a village, houses were spaced in a reasonable manner. Some houses had tule mats hung in the doorway to act as a screen from the wind. The floor was bare dirt or sometimes beach sand. The earthen floor was hardened from use and could be kept relatively clean. The door to the house was positioned to the west or to the sea, to keep away the sharp, north wind.

This type of house was quickly and easily built and quite sound, able to keep even the coldest winter at bay. Tule thatch up to half a foot thick provided excellent insulation. In time, when damage became great, either by insect pests or weather it could easily be torched and a clean, new domicile built.

On the Islands, where trees and thatching material were scarce some of the structural elements were made from whale bones or manzanita branches. At least one early explorer reports seeing large houses on Santa Catalina Island.

The sweat house was another structure found in a typical Gabrielino village. The Spanish called them *temescales*. The *temescal* was used often. It was a pleasure which these people clearly relished for its rejuvenating effects. *Temescales* were made of wooden boughs and were coated with mud. There was little smoke when the *temescal* was in use, because the fire was carefully tended and stoked with dry, flammable willow twigs. Hunters used the sweat house to mask all traces of their human scent allowing them to sneak up on large game unnoticed.

Clearly the Gabrielino deeply appreciated the sense of stability and comfort provided by a permanent and well-furnished home, where family groups could live together and share the same hearth. The very fact that the Gabrielino were able to settle in one place and remain for a number of years added to the richness of their culture and allowed for a way of life that cultivated the easy transference of traditional values.

Thatched Gabrielino domicile. Photograph Bruce W. Miller. LACNHM.

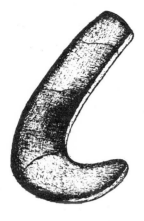

TRADE

TRADE WAS A COMMONPLACE activity for the Gabrielino. A regional economy and network of trading sites and trails developed throughout Southern California, directly linking many tribes, some as far away as the Mojave desert. The amount of goods traded was substantial and there were set times for trading to take place. The Gabrielino and the Chumash both sustained viable economies primarily because they supplied much of the shell-bead money used throughout Southern California.

Shell bead money was made from olivella shells which were broken into small roundish pieces of roughly similar size, drilled with a chert drill and then strung on fiber string or sinew. The beads were then rounded to a uniform size by scraping the strung pieces of shell back on forth on a sandstone surface. The standard unit of measure in Gabrielino territory and much of the Southern California was a string of beads wrapped once around the hand.

The Gabrielino villages traded among themselves and barter for goods was sophisticated. There were standardized sizes and quality of tradegoods to facilitate the exchange. Trading helped to increase the diversity of goods available in any one area. Goods that were common on the coast might be scarce or unavailable inland, therefore trade was not only opportunistic but necessary. This routine trading of surplus articles, encouraged craft specialization (shell money and steatite mining) which led to manufacturing sites on the coast and the Islands.

Between the Island and the mainland Gabrielino trade thrived. Goods traveling from the Islands to the mainland were beads, shell jewelry, steatite, digging-stick weights, ollas, sea otter and seal skins. In turn, the Islanders got acorns, pinenuts, chia seeds, islay, deer and rabbit skins, and obsidian points.

There was also trading between villages up and down the coast. Gabrielino traders would travel the coast in their canoes, meeting at preselected spots. The Gabrielino would travel north with trade goods for the Chumash who were particularly fond of steatite for bowls, pipes and effigies.

The Inland Gabrielino would come to the coast frequently, to trade for fresh and dried fish, shellfish, steatite and other necessities from the coastal craft industries.

The Mojave, a tribe that inhabited the desert regions of inland California near the Colorado River, would make a two-week trip over the mountains into Gabrielino territory to trade. They brought black, woven cotton for blankets, fire-hardened pottery, and small balls of bright-red hematite that the Gabrielino particularly liked for body painting and decorating everyday objects. In return the Gabrielino gave them shell beads, steatite and asphaltum.

Shell beads attached to top of a hairpin or awl. Courtesy Antelope Valley Indian Museum.

Shell bead money. Note relative uniformity. Courtesy Antelope Valley Indian Museum.

Small mortar and pestle (two inches) and two thimble sized paint mortars. Top and bottom photos courtesy Antelope Valley Indian Museum.

Small paint mortar and pestle with hematite (iron oxide paint) still in it.

 # *LOOKING BACKWARD*

MOST GABRIELINO CULTURAL tradition has long since vanished under the great concrete and asphalt expanse that is now modern Los Angeles. But there is a subtle, and pervasive influence of these magnificent people amongst us everyday, if only in place-names such as Cucamonga, Topanga, and Tuhunga. In many ways Gabrielino culture is alive, even today. There are any number of Gabrielino people who maintain some of their ancient traditions, living in the Los Angeles area and elsewhere.

The complexity of Gabrielino culture was underestimated, or simply ignored, from the first European contact. The Spanish were more interested in conquering and converting the native, Southern California population than in learning from them. They had an almost-total disregard for native, cultural values. Fortunately for us, there was a tradition among these Europeans of travel writing and it is from these all-too-scarce sources that information on Gabrielino culture has come down to us. What knowledge we have comes from ships logs, "diaries of the voyage," personal diaries and letter writing.

Hugo Reid, for example was particularly sensitive to the need for the preservation of information about these people, even as he watched their destruction. Reid was married to a Gabrielino woman.

Still, there exists a whole panoply of problems in reconstructing a true and living picture of Gabrielino culture, much of which was lost to us before anyone thought to record any of the details. The Gabrielino were singularly unfortunate in this regard. Most of their culture disappeared very quickly. The tribes surrounding them were slightly more fortunate. The Cahuilla, Lusieño, and Chumash sustained remnants of their cultures longer than the Gabrielino, but just barely. Many tribes that occupied what is modern-day Southern California had disparate ethnography but similar material culture. The Chumash to the north of the Gabrielino, for example were remarkably similar in material culture and yet vastly different in other things.

Environment as a cultural factor should not be overlooked either. Climate, geography, flora, fauna and available water all directly relate to the way in which the Gabrielino lived and the manner in which they believed. The mild climate and relatively abundant food supply along the coastal plain bordering the Pacific, for example, while supporting the development and diversity of tribes and dialects in the area, also supported the unity and permanence of cultural patterns and values.

Another problem in defining aspects of Gabrielino culture include the passage of time, as well as our own cultural differences from these peoples. There are tremendous gaps in our knowledge and we may never have the whole picture. And finally there are our own expectations and romance with native cultures, which can obscure the fact that at times the life of the Gabrielino must have been a harsh, even brutal existence.

Nevertheless, the long process of reconstructing the past has begun. We know some of it. There is still more to learn.

Gabrielino rock painting. Courtesy Southwest Museum.

Multicolored rock painting attributed to both Chumash and Gabrielino. Courtesy Southwest Museum

LIFEWAYS

THE LIFE OF THE GABRIELINO was centered around the household and in turn, the village. Food was brought to the village site to be prepared and then consumed with the excess put into storage. The Gabrielino built large thatched dwellings, occupied by extended family groups. In the larger villages, the houses, while made of relatively perishable materials, were well maintained. Inside, the houses were spacious and comfortable with a fire in the center of the room. Reed mats were hung from the ceiling, as curtains to make a partitioned room.

When not spending time hunting, gathering and preparing food, the Gabrielino were playing games, gambling, sunbathing, preparing for rituals and solstice celebrations, manufacturing basketry, tools and trade materials and making personal adornments. The majority of wooden artifacts—bowls, mortars, bows and arrows and canoes have been destroyed. Nevertheless, the few extant examples demonstrate the rich and varied life the Gabrielino led.

Along the coast, near present day Long Beach, the Gabrielino were most numerous. Many villages were permanently occupied although their population may have varied with the season depending on food resources. Up and down the coast ranged twenty or thirty villages. some as large a 500 inhabitants and many thatched houses. Estuaries and sloughs at the mouths of creeks or small rivers in the area were favorite coastal village sites. On the Islands particularly Santa Catalina, the villages tended to be near the shoreline rather than the mountainous interior. The Inland Gabrielino living in an arid region and at a higher altitude built their villages along the small rivers and creeks.

Large or small, villages were planned around the same principles. Pathways leading between houses formed a kind of street. Other important features of the village were the Chief's house, the storehouse or granary which might be located near the Chief's house, or in a dry, well-trafficked area away from rodents.

Much of what we know about the Gabrielino comes from two sources. Hugo Reid, as mentioned before and Father Geronimo Boscana, in his *Historical Account of San Juan Capistrano Indians of Southern California*. Father Boscana was stationed at San Juan Capistrano from 1812 to 1826. Before he died at San Gabriel mission he completed this most important document on Southern California Indian life.

Mission San Juan Capistrano was in Lusieño territory but the best experts believe that many of Lusieño lifeways were similar to the Gabrielino. It is thought that the main tenets of Lusieño religion, *Chinigchinix*, were in fact learned from the Gabrielino.

DAILY LIFE.

When a Gabrielino man wanted to become married, he would court his chosen bride by walking back and forth in front of her house, waiting for a chance to speak with her. He would not enter the house but when his chance came to speak with his intended he would say, "I want to marry you" Sometimes a third party was sent for, to take the girl in hand and get her consent. If she agreed to get married to the man then she would speak with her parents. After, if the parents were in agreement with his proposal, the young man would come inside the house, bringing her presents, perhaps sea otter fur, shell-beads, deerskin, or even seeds. If all agreed, there would be a match then the perspective bride and groom would do their duties: the woman would clean the house and prepare food while the man would hunt rabbits or other game. This period of betrothal would last about two weeks. In this time the pair would become acquainted with each other. Soon, the relatives and the rest of the *rancheria* were notified and a great feast was held. Then the pair were considered married (Harrington:1934,23).

When a woman became pregnant, another feast was held. At birth, the baby was cleaned off and shown around the village as the newest member of the tribe. Also, just before, during and after childbirth both the mother and the father would be confined to the house and go on a special diet. Generally no meat was eaten during this time.

As a child grew he/she would be instructed in the ways of the tribe. When males were six or seven years of age a supernatural spirit would choose them. This animal spirit, sometimes manifested in a personal talisman, would defend them from "all dangers especially in wars against their enemies" (Harrington:1934,17).

For the youngest initiates, a drink prepared from native tobacco was given. At an older age, a shaman would begin a similar ceremony by administering, *toloache*, a hallucinatory drink made from jimson weed (*Datura wrightii*), to his young subject. This alkali based poison, (scopolamine and atropine), induced a hallucinatory, dream state, either waking or coma-like during which a person would meet by sign, or by recognition his dream helper. The subject would be made to fast from three or four days. During all of this time he would be instructed by the village elders.

As children, girls were given much the same instruction as boys. There was also a custom of tattooing girls between the eyebrows. Many women later added more lattice or lined tattoos.

Among the Gabrielino were shamans. These men were highly respected, even feared, by ordinary people. They also held great political and religious power. The shamans ability to interpret the environment was especially valuable to the Gabrielino who saw their world in a constant state of flux. Shamans were intensely interested and aware of the movement of the cosmos. Their immediate concern was the continued balance and proper alignment of the forces of the universe. To tap into the power ot the cosmos, they explored esoteric knowledge, celebrated the heavenly bodies, and performed sacred rituals. These rituals closely followed the phases of the moon, as well as, the rising, setting and declination of the sun. The shamans ability to interpret their environment was vitally important to the Gabrielino.

Many California Indian tribes made use of charmstones—small cylindrical stones with tapered ends, rather like plummet stones. The Gabrielino were no exception and their charmstones were usually made from steatite, or sandstone. Gabrielino shamans used these ritual objects for a variety of purposes, including curing the sick, for sorcery, and for manipulating the weather.

Shamans might also employ large quartz crystals which were sometimes attached to wands. Other talismans included various animal parts, teeth, bird talons, bits of human hair.

The ritual paraphernalia of the Shaman bears some examination. Generally, he would possess a number of talismans and other symbols to denote his station and powers. One interesting implement was the sun staff. This was a perforated stone mounted on a wooden staff. Henry Henshaw, in his article of 1877, *Perforated Stones of California* described their origins and probable use. *After careful consideration of these implements I am convinced that their peculiarities accord best with the idea that they were the property of medicine men or conjurers, probably used in dances or ceremonies, as rain making, curing the sick etc, (Henshaw, 1877:30, 31).*

These steatite stones that surmounted the sun staff were often incised with rays, or geometric designs representing the declination of the sun, or the cardinal points of the Gabrielino compass. The Chumash used these sunstaffs in the all-important solstice ceremony where the shaman would tap the stone three times and then symbolically pull the sun back in a northward direction, signifying the end of winter and the beginning of the sun's return.

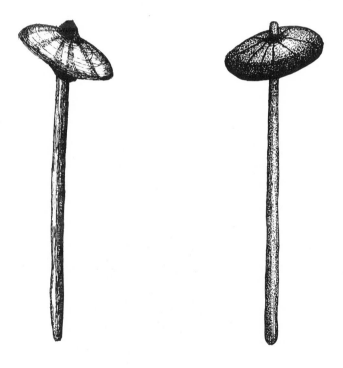

Sun staff. Wooden staff surmounted by a perforated steatite disk. The incised markings on the top edge of the stone are thought to mark the inclination of the sun and or the cardinal points of the compass.

Shamans served many vital functions in the life of the Gabrielino, but were also viewed with some ambivalence. Ordinary people feared their power. They were specialists using their esoteric skills in various, specific disciplines. They were present at births and deaths. Shamans named children, predicted the future and influenced the course and nature of the weather. They cured illness by blowing sacred smoke, by singing, by dancing and by ritual use of herbs. They were diviners and sorcerers; some could be possessed by a bear spirit which would give them great strength and allow them congress with bears. They could travel abroad, moving between realms and around the world, with supernatural ability. Above all they possessed a superior ability to control external events.

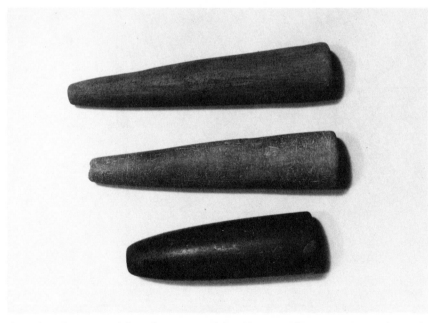

Steatite pipes. Used for pleasure and by Shaman doctors to cure the sick. Photograph by Bruce W. Miller, Courtesy Antelope Valley Indian Museum.

Steatite pipe with bird bone stem.

One of the most important occupations among shamans was that of doctor or *medicine man*. Experienced with datura, curative tree bark and medicinal herbs, these shaman-doctors would treat the ill by summoning powers and sucking the disease from the patient's body by means of a steatite, or bird-bone tube. The shaman would place feathers around the patient and make small gestures, speaking words that only he knew. He would then place the bone, or steatite medicine tube over the painful area sucking the cause of the disease from the patient's body.

Native medicine was holistic in nature and reasonably effective. External sores, tumors, swelling and other diseases were treated with herbs and poultices. Sometimes, stinging nettle was applied to the infected part of the body. Internal illness was treated by inhaling smoke or by eating herbs. In some cases fasting, warmwater springs, the temescal, or even cold water were used effectively.

When a person died, the shaman would prepare the body for cremation and burial. The corpse would be laid out for half a day, to make sure that the person was dead. A pyre was prepared by the cremator, a person who was assigned this task.

Father Boscana described this ceremony in his account of the Indians at San Juan Capistrano:

Everything being ready, they carried the corpse to the pyre, leaving it there. All the people withdrew to a little distance, the cremator alone remaining. He lighted the pyre, and he could not stir from the place until the dead person was entirely consumed. And when it was over they gave him something to eat, and paid him well, and after that he retired to his lodging place.

All the things and utensils which the dead person had used, such as bows, arrows, feathers, and the rest were all burned with him, serving as food for the pyre. They did not have special ceremonies at the time of the burning him, but after he was entirely consumed, they retired to a little distance from the rancheria to cry over the death of the deceased (Harrington, 1934:50).

This *killing* of a person's possessions was thought to complete the burial. Ritual destruction was necessary, because of their belief that the power of these objects was of no use to anyone else. While many of the Southern California Indians were materialistic, they practiced this *killing* of objects, because of their strong belief in the spiritual nature of the world. The power of an object depended on many things, not just the skill of its maker. Every object was connected to the spiritual world and was empowered by the spirit within it.

 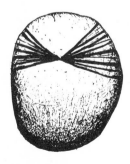

Gaming or ceremonial stones. Flat, pendant sized rocks marked with brown paint. Courtesy Southwest Museum

Steatite and chalcedony (m.) charmstones. Used by Shaman to predict the future and change the weather. Antelope Valley Indian Museum

Cog stone fetish. Courtesy Antelope Valley Indian Museum.

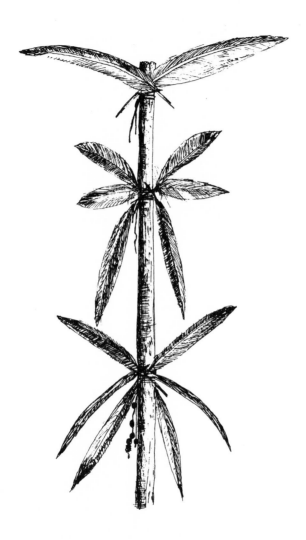

Feathered pole. These shrines were erected on natural mounds to protect crops or placed in accordance with summer and winter solstice ceremonies.

Ritual paint dish with shell bead inlay on exterior of rim. (one inch diameter) Courtesy Antelope Valley Indian Museum.

*Cog stone.
These stones were
found in many
parts of the
Los Angeles Basin
They have been linked
to ritual practices.
Photograph by
Bruce W. Miller
Courtesy Los Angeles
County Natural
History Museum.*

Brush of soapwood root with asphaltum handle.(top) Whale bone imple-
ment or chisel. (bottom) Courtesy Southwest Museum.

Round gaming stone. Courtesy Antelope Valley Museum

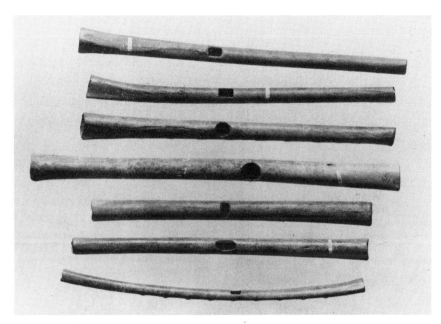

Bone whistles. They produce a high shrill sound. Courtesy Collection of Mr. J. A. Barro & Southwest Museum.

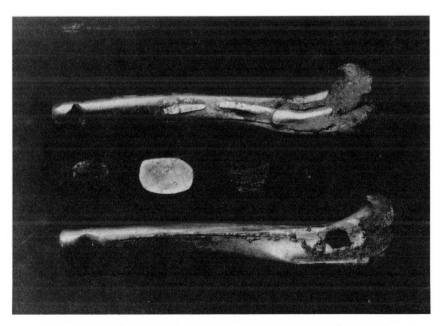

Deer tibia whistles from San Nicolàs Is. Courtesy Southwest Museum.

The Gabrielino were a fun-loving people who set much store in music dancing and games. They were avid gamblers, especially the women who would play for shell bead money, tossing dice across a flat coiled-basket tray. Music served as simple entertainment, or more significantly, as an accompaniment to the religious dances at festivals. Guests were often entertained by dancing and music.

The Gabrielino had a few favorite instruments. Flutes and whistle were numerous and made of bone, wood and cane. Whistles were made from the tibia (lower leg bone) of deer, from mountain lion bones, or from hollow, bird bones. Sometimes they were bound together like pan pipes to produce several tones from the same instrument. These pan pipes and other whistles were sometimes decorated with asphaltum and shell beads, or incised with geometric patterns. They were sometimes suspended with fiber string from the neck (Hudson & Blackburn 1986:349).

The Gabrielino made a number of percussive type instruments. These included: bullroarers (a small, flat board attached to a long cord that is swung around in the air over the head to make a low, buzzing sound which resonates for a great distance; tap sticks (two sticks which when struck together, make a clacking sound); split stick clappers which, when shaken in the air correctly will produce a sharp clapping sound; and rattles of various types.

From archaeological evidence and the earliest historical sources, it is clear that the Gabrielino were very fine craftspeople. They excelled in many areas—basketry, tool making, and boat building, to name the most obvious. They were clever at exploiting their environment, and utilized sandstone, steatite, wood, grass, animal hides, seashells, bones, chert, asphaltum, and just about anything else that was serviceable.

Much of what the Gabrielino people used has not survived, with the exception of things made of stone, shell and bone. For the most part, perishable items such as baskets are in museums and private collections and date from the Mission period.

Other woven, or feathered artifacts, headdresses, skirts, and fish nets are fewer and very scarce. Even so, some of the Gabrielino heritage has survived into our time. Such is the beauty and tragedy of this fine people.

BIBLIOGRAPHY

Bancroft, Hubert Howe. *The Works of Hubert Howe Bancroft, Volume XVIII, History of California Vol. I 1542-1800.* San Francisco: A. L. Bancroft.1884.

Batman, Richard. *The Outer Coast.* New York: Harcourt Brace Jovanovich, 1985.

Bean, Walton. *California, An Interpretive History.* 2nd ed. New York: McGraw-Hill, 1973.

Bolton, Herbert Eugene. *Spanish Exploration in the Southwest.* New York: Scribners,1908.

. Fray Juan Crespí, *Missionary Explorer on the Pacific Coast 1769-1774.* Berkeley: UCB, 1927.

. editor, *Historical Memoirs of New California, Francisco Palou.* Berkeley: University of California Press, 1926.

. *Anza's California Expeditions.* Berkeley: University of California Press, 1930.

Bryan, Bruce. *Archaeological Explorations on San Nicolas Island.* Los Angeles: Southwest Museum, 1970.

Cunningham, Richard W., *California Indian Watercraft*. San Luis Obispo: EZ Nature Books, 1989.

Davis, James T. *Trade Routes and Economic Exchange Among the Indians of California*. Ramona: Ballena Press, 1974.

Dawson L. & Deetz, J. *A Corpus of Chumash Basketry*, Los Angeles, University of California, 1965.

Denis, Alberta Johnson. *Spanish Alta California*. New York: Macmillan, 1927.

Ebeling, Walter. *Handbook of Indian Foods and Fibers of Arid America*. Berkeley: University of California Press, 1986.

Engelhardt, Zephyrin. *San Gabriel Mission and the Beginnings of Los Angeles*. San Gabriel: Mission San Gabriel, 1927.

Geiger, Maynard J. *The Life and Times of Fray Junipero Serra, O. F. M.* Washington: Academy of American Franciscan History, 1959.

Grant, Campbell. *The Rock Paintings of the Chumash Indians*. Berkeley, University of California Press, 1965.

Harrington, John Peabody. *Cultural Element Distributions: XIX Central California Coast. Antrpological Records Vol. 7, No.1.* Berkeley: UNiversity of California Press, 1942.

Heizer, Robert F. *Handbook of the North American Indians. California Volume 8.* Washington: Smithsonian Institution, 1978.

. & Elsasser, Albert B. *Original Accounts of the Lone Woman of San Nicolas Island*. Berkeley: University of California Berkely, 1961.

Hudson, Dee T. *Chumash Archery Equipment*. San Diego: San Diego Museum of Man, 1974.

Hudson, Travis & Blackburn, Thomas C. 1982-1987. *The Material Culture of the Chumash Interaction Sphere, Volumes 1-5.* Menlo Park: Ballena Press, 1982-1987.

Hudson, Travis, et al., *Tomol: Chumash Water as Described in the Ethnographic Notes of John P. Harrington.* Menlo Park:Ballena Press, 1978

Johnston, Bernice Eastman. *California's Gabrielino Indians.* Los Angeles: Southwest Museum, 1962.

Kroeber, A. L. *Handbook of the Indians of California.* New York: Dover Publications, 1976.

Mathes, W. Michael. *Vizcaino, and Spanish Expansion in the Pacific Ocean 1580-1630.* San Francisco: California Historical Society, 1968.

Miller, Bruce W. *Chumash, A Picture of Their World.* Los Osos: Sand River Press, 1987.

Moriarty, James Robert. *Chinigchinix, An Indigenous California Indian Religion.* Los Angeles, Southwest Museum, 1969.

Teggart, Frederick J. *The Anza Expedition of 1775-1776. Diary of Pedro Font.* Berkeley: UCB, 1913.

Terrell, John Upton. *The Arrow and the Cross, A History of the American Indian and the Missionaries.* Santa Barbara: Capra Press, 1979.

Turnbaugh, Sarah Peabody. *Indian Baskets.* West Chester: Schiffer Publishing, 1986.

Walker, Edwin Francis. *Five Prehistoric Archaeological Sites In Los Angeles County, California.* Los Angeles: Southwest Museum, 1951.

Wlodarski, Robert J. *Catalina Island Soapstone Manufacture. Journal of California and Great Basin Anthropology Vol. 1, No.2 pp 331-355.* (1979)

INDEX

Other Books from **SAND RIVER PRESS**, 1319, 14th Street, Los Osos, CA., 93402. Please send $1.50 shipping and handling and California residents please add 7.25% sales tax.

Chumash, A Picture of Their World. Bruce W. Miller. $8.95, Trade paperback. ISBN 0-944627-51-X. 145 pages. A popular history of the Chumash Indian tribe. Illustrated with many black and white photographs and drawings. Bruce W. Miller has written the best popular guide to this enduring California Indian tribe.

With Steinbeck in the Sea of Cortez. Sparky Enea and Audry Lynch. ISBN 0-944627-56-0. A memoir of the Steinbeck/Ricketts expedition to Baja California as told by fellow crew member, Sparky Enea. He tells true tales of Cannery Row, "Doc" Ricketts and writer John Steinbeck. Follow Sparky to La Paz and Guaymas, through days and nights of madcap marine specimen collecting as he and the rest of the crew of the *Western Flyer* make literary history. Illustrated with black and white photographs of the trip.

Finding My Way, A Journey Round the Rim of the Catholic Worker Movement. Toni Flynn. $7.95 Trade paperback. ISBN 0-944627-35-8. 100 pages. A personal look at salvation and the Catholic Worker Movement. Essays. Toni Flynn is deeply involved in helping the poor and hungry. Here is a moving look at her first hand experiences with helping people save themselves.

Rivers of the Heart. George DeBord. $9.95, Trade paperback. ISBN 0-944627-33-1 Essays and Memoirs on the the West, including California, Nebraska, Wyoming, Kansas, Oregon and Missouri. DeBord Writes from a compelling sense of place to create lingering visions of the West. Here are the lakes and rivers and small towns come alive.